THE WOMAN'S GUIDE TO Selling Residential Real Estate Successfully

Also by Carolyn Janik

•

THE HOUSE HUNT GAME

A GUIDE TO WINNING

SELLING YOUR HOME

A GUIDE TO GETTING THE BEST PRICE
WITH OR WITHOUT A BROKER

THE WOMAN'S GUIDE TO *Selling Residential Real Estate Successfully*

A STEP-BY-STEP CAREER PROGRAM

by

CAROLYN JANIK

NEW YORK EVEREST HOUSE PUBLISHERS

Library of Congress Cataloging in Publication Data:

Janik, Carolyn.

The woman's guide to selling residential real estate successfully.

Includes index.

1. Real estate business—Vocational guidance.
2. Women in real estate. 3. Real estate agents.
4. House selling. I. Title.

HD1382.J35 333.33'023'73 81-3168

ISBN: 0-89696-131-1 AACR2

Published simultaneously in Canada by
Beaverbooks, Don Mills, Ontario
Manufactured in the United States of America
Designed by Abe Lerner
First Edition RRD981

FOR KATHY KAINER

•

Friendship is a warming fire

In a world of winter winds

ACKNOWLEDGMENTS

My appreciation and gratitude are sincerely extended to Sandra Arden, Richard Balkin, Jerry Gross, Lillian McClintock, and Joseph Janik, each of whom helped give life to this book.

CONTENTS

INTRODUCTION

A Personal Note

IT ALL began for me with a folded piece of paper passed across the aisle in Ed. 403. "Do you know anyone who wants to sell real estate?" it read. "Allied Brokers needs people and is offering a free training program."

Glancing at my note-passing acquaintance, I shook my head. "Not me!" I thought. I was bound for a Masters in education and a quiet, secure career teaching English.

But six months later I was scanning the pages of my Ed. 403 notebook for the name and phone number of the woman who passed that note. I still thought of myself as an English teacher, but I needed money and I had become interested in real estate.

In the innocence of our twenties, my husband and I had bought a piece of land with a sizable short-term mortgage held by the seller. The lot had 194 feet of lake frontage and we had dreams of building a castle that would be reflected in the clear water of the lake and shaded by the stately trees around it. Ummmmmmmm, yes. We also had a $1,000 payment due in three months and no foreseeable way of getting the money. Now that I was a landowner, it occurred to me that maybe I *could* sell real estate. Maybe it was the high-paying job that I could juggle, along with the care of my two preschool children and my one-course-a-semester trek toward that Master's degree.

Does that sound insane to you? It does to me now, too, and it must have to my future employer as he sat behind his desk and listened to me tell it. But he was opening a new office in the very town where I lived and he was desperate for agents to open the doors each morning and answer the phones. I got the job, if you can call it that. There was no pay, only the promise of a fifty-fifty commission split *if* I sold or listed successfully.

What did he have to lose, really? And what did I gain really, except heavier, tighter time pressure on that due date three months away and the added expense of baby-sitting fees for my children. I was so green that I didn't know that most houses take from two to three months to close and that no one gets paid until after the closing. I didn't know that I would have to sell a house or two almost immediately in order to have the money for our land payment. And I didn't know how hard it was to sell a house or two! "Fools walk in . . ."

I asked about the "free training program." "Later," he said. He handed me a thick green book and told me to study for the licensing exam. It was scheduled for next week, he said, and if I drove up to Hartford that day I could file my application in time. I did it and spent the next week of my life intimately involved with *Questions and Answers on Real Estate* by Robert Semenow. (Still in print and now a million-copy best seller!) There was no class hour requirement before taking the licensing exam in Connecticut at the time (there is now) and with great good luck, I passed.

So I began work. I had a license coming in the mail, a well-memorized vocabulary of real estate and legal terms, a desk, a phone, and tremendous motivation. I began by calling every for-sale-by-owner ad in the newspaper and trying to talk whoever answered the phone into listing with my agency. After a while my ear began to hurt, my rejection tolerance was worn gossamer thin, and I had reached the last column of the houses-for-sale section of the classifieds. And then, unbelievably, there was a woman who would talk with me, who even seemed interested, and finally who agreed to allow me to come to see her home.

Was I surprised when the couple nodded to each other and said they would give me the listing? Just a bit. I hadn't even remembered to take along the listing form! And my boss was a bit surprised, too, when I called and asked if he would run them over to me.

It was unheard of, taking a listing on the first day of work, but that was nothing when compared to how I sold that same house a week later. It happened in a barber shop.

My five-year-old was getting his hair cut and I was making

conversation with the barber. "Do you know anyone who wants to buy a really beautiful bi-level?" I asked.

"You selling your house?" he asked in return.

"No, I just got a job as a real estate agent," I replied, "and I listed this fabulous house."

It wasn't a fabulous house at all, but I guess it sounded like a fabulous house as I described it, for a man sitting in the corner put down his newspaper and said, "You know that sounds like a perfect house for an employee I've got coming into this area." He took my name and phone number and the address of the property. I told him I was holding an Open House on Sunday afternoon. He said his man would be there.

He was. In fact, he and his wife were the only two people who came to that Open House. And they bought it.

My share of the listing and selling commission was $1,275. Enough to make our land payment and get me started on a career.

To this day it was my easiest sale. Since then I've seen a deal fall apart at the closing table over some appliances; a seller with a heart attack one week before closing; buyers who changed their minds after signing contracts and lost their deposit monies; corporate transferees who needed to find (and found) a house in three days; buyers who ran me around for months and then quietly bought privately; deals that could not be made because there was a thousand dollars difference in price and no one would budge; mortgage applications that fell through; checks that bounced; sellers who concealed everything from leaky basements to liens on their properties; buyers who lied about income and outstanding debts; sellers who took everything out of their houses when moving including the mailbox, the light bulbs, and the toilet-paper rollers; other agents who spied and lied to steal a customer or a listing; brokers who "miscalculated" my earnings; a seller who threatened me with a broom because she didn't like the offer I brought to her—the list of stories could fill a long evening.

After that first deal, I really did take Allied Brokers' free training course, and several others as well, along with a formal licensing course in another state. I've heard the "should-be-dones" and "can-go-wrongs" and seen examples of most of them. And I've learned that most of this job isn't *taught,* it's learned. Usually through experience and usually that experience is expensive.

And that brings me to the purpose of this book. It is a sharing of my experiences in the residential marketplace. It is not for women who run large brokerage firms; others who specialize in property management or rentals; others in commercial real estate; others in appraisal. As for the many men in real estate, I welcome them to read my words, of course, but I wrote this book for the vast majority of women in real estate who sell houses, and for every woman who has considered a career in real estate and would like an inside look before making a commitment.

THE WOMAN'S GUIDE TO Selling Residential Real Estate Successfully

ONE

It's a Job

WOULD it surprise you to know that an estimated 40 percent of beginning real estate sales people drop out of the business before the end of their *first year*? Another 20 percent by the end of their second year? And that less than 30 percent of those beginners are still working in the field after five years? What happens to these people? What is it about the job that attracts so many and then turns so very many away?

There has never been a formal study to answer those questions, but I'm willing to hazard some guesses. Some of the dropouts learned a lot, some wasted a good deal of time and money. They were originally attracted to real estate sales because it seemed to offer a pleasant kind of work; or a professional status; or a flexibility of work schedule; or the opportunity to earn high income; or the chance to be their own boss; or because they needed a job and someone told them XYZ Real Estate was hiring. They left because they didn't like the work or because they were not successful at it.

But these statements could be made to a greater or lesser degree about many careers. Why then are the percentages of dropouts so very high in real estate? The answer, I believe, has to do with image. Almost everyone who has ever bought or sold property thinks that he or she knows exactly what the job of a real estate agent is. In reality, however, home buyers or sellers know only the equivalent of a concert pianist's performance or an actor's appearance on stage. They do not know the study, training, preparation, and just plain hard work that is the *real* job. And believe me, it's a job, a job with all the highs and lows, pros and cons, benefits and detriments of any other job, and a few unique ones too.

But let me introduce you to that job before we talk about how to be successful at it. I'd like to begin with an overview, a kind of aerial wide-angle photo of life as a woman in real estate. Those of you who've been in the business a while will recognize a lot of familiar landmarks; those of you who are new, or have not yet begun, may find some surprises in the picture.

SHOWING HOUSES

My best real estate day was when our whole office went to visit a listing my broker had taken. The property was a small estate and the house was an exact duplicate of the Admiral Byrd house in Washington, D.C. Every room brought new delights: carved cherry paneling in the library; dental moldings at the ceilings; imported Dutch tiles around the fireplace in the master bedroom; hand stenciled Early American motifs on the walls; Belgian mirrors; Oriental rugs; oil paintings; ceramic floors; even a temperature-controlled and well-stocked wine cellar. I returned home delighted, a little awed, and bubbling with aesthetic appreciation.

But such days are very rare indeed. Many women think they would enjoy real estate sales as a career because they have enjoyed being homemakers. They have made curtains, chosen paint and wallpaper, co-ordinated furniture and fabrics and carpeting, and generally transformed houses into homes. They take pride in those homes and they are genuinely appreciative of the decorating and good taste in the other homes that they visit. These women often think of a real estate agent as a person who shows houses, and the thought of seeing and showing the interiors of hundreds of houses a year is very appealing to them.

Unfortunately, showing houses is only a small part of the job and not nearly as pleasant as most people imagine. Oh, you do see many lovely homes and sometimes you do get some great decorating ideas, but a home quickly becomes a house when you are walking through every room—upstairs to the bedrooms and downstairs to the cellar—and twice around the outside for the fifth time with your fifth different customer.

And on days when you show three houses to one customer in the morning and four houses to another customer in the afternoon, you come back to your own home too tired to care about wallpaper, and drapes, and furniture arrangement. Your place is not quite as clean as you would like it, your dinner is less than elegant, but it all seems pretty much OK in comparison to what you have been showing all day.

The fact is that most houses are more or less ordinary. Estates and decorator specials are the exceptions, the high points of your week (or month). As a working agent, the glossy appeal of showing houses wears away quickly. You come to expect the standard floor plans for a ranch, or a split-level, or a colonial, and the traditional arrangements of furniture in a family room, the conventional wallpapers in bedrooms and bathrooms and kitchens. Houses become for the real estate agent something like the heavy fabric sample books interior decorators lug about with them—a very necessary part of the job.

LOOKING AT HOUSES

A good residential agent spends almost as much time looking at houses as showing them. The majority of agents today work for brokers who are Realtors and members of Multiple Listing boards. The larger the board, the larger the number of new listings each week. These listings must be seen in person to be effectively discussed with customers, which means that pre-inspection visits and Realtor Open Houses occupy several hours each week.

Sometimes these pre-inspection visits are very quick run-throughs, just enough to get an idea of floor plan and something to talk with a customer about. Other times the pre-inspection is the agent's opportunity to check out the condition and quality of a house, to look for termites and water problems, to evaluate heating and plumbing efficiency, to estimate property boundary lines, and generally find the answers to the questions her customers will probably ask. This kind of careful work takes time, but it is time well spent in building your competence and self-confidence. It will also stand you in good stead when a customer says, "Gee, I wonder what it costs to heat this place," and you immediately reply, "The owner's heating bill last year was $730."

LOOKING FOR HOUSES

One broker with whom I worked used to say "Real estate is the only profession I know where, when you run low on stock, you just go out and find some more." He was referring of course to listings. Every experienced agent knows that listing houses is every bit as important, and as lucrative, as selling houses.

In fact there is intense competition among brokers for more and better listings in every town and every city in the country. Listings are the backbone of an effectively run office; without listings there is nothing to advertise and therefore no easy way to get new customers. Every broker urges his staff to list, and every agent knows that getting good listings requires not only a little effort, but also stamina and perseverance.

A top agent reads the houses-for-sale classified ads of the local papers every day looking for new for-sale-by-owner inserts. She calls these people, or better yet she goes to visit their properties. When she is welcomed, she inspects the house with the owners and often spends time telling them about her office and its staff and services. Often she returns a second time with comparables (listings similar to the property in question that have been sold during the past year) to give the sellers a competitive market analysis. And sometimes she returns a third time to take the listing, measure rooms, and collect tax information, exact lot dimensions, and a myriad of other specifics necessary for a thorough and professional property description. Sometimes she will take photos of both the interior and exterior.

Besides newspaper ads, leads for listings often come from referrals, old customers, friends or community acquaintances, divorce and estate lawyers, and canvassing. When the response to your knock on the door is "No, we're not interested," a looking-for-houses expedition takes the time it took to get the address of the property, drive to it, and drive back to the office. The good leads—those where your knock is answered with an invitation to come into the living room—take anywhere from one hour to several hours, depending on how close you come to taking that listing.

CANVASSING

I don't know a single real estate agent who enjoys canvassing. There are two kinds, phone and door-to-door. The objective in both is to introduce yourself to a homeowner (sometimes with a give-away like a potholder or Frisbee imprinted with the agency name), talk about your office, and find out if that homeowner or anyone he or she knows is planning to move in the near future.

It is difficult, discouraging, and sometimes even embarrassing work, but statistical studies show that it does get results and more and more of the large independent Realtor firms and the giant franchise members are requiring that their sales agents spend some time each week canvassing.

FLOOR TIME

Most new customers (and therefore most sales) come to an office through walk-in response to the agency sign on the street or phone response to advertising. Most offices therefore divide the work day into shifts in which individual agents are responsible for answering any phone inquiries on ads or assisting anyone who comes into the office looking to buy or list. The length of these shifts and their frequency within the week varies from one office to another depending upon its size and procedural policies, but almost everywhere floor time means that an agent is expected to be in the office and that all new business generated during that time will be hers. If she is out of the office during her floor time, she forfeits its business to the agent who covers for her.

Very often nothing happens during floor time. The phone calls are for other members of the staff or business calls not related to new customers, and no one new comes in the door. Often it's a time to catch up on paperwork, the mortgage market, phone canvassing, and new listings. It is also a time to hope that one of the incoming calls will have a ready, willing, and able customer on the other end of the line.

PAPERWORK

You can't show or sell a house that's already sold or one that you don't know is for sale. Which means, in trade jargon, you must keep up with the market. Which means paperwork.

Keeping pace with the day-to-day happenings of the residential marketplace can be a real test of skill and efficiency, especially in the busy spring and fall seasons in most parts of the country. On some of the largest multiple listing boards, weekly computer print-out books update new listings, price changes, and recent sales, thus eliminating much filing and revision work. But even on these boards, daily bulletins—or flash sheets as they are sometimes called—are issued with information on newly listed properties, price changes, and deposits taken. An agent must post this information daily into her computer-printed listing book. Ignoring the flash sheets may mean that a new listing, perfect for one of your customers, is sold before it comes out in next week's book, or that someone else gets the bargain of a price-reduced property, or that you take customers to a property, knock at the door, and face an owner who snarls, "It was sold two days ago."

On smaller boards, individual listing sheets on each property come through at various intervals from daily to weekly. These sheets must be filed by town and price in your own set of listing binders. Along with the new listing sheets come lists of deposits taken; price changes; additional information or changes of information on specified houses; deletions; renewals; and the actual selling price of houses that have closed. Most of this information is essential and must be added to each listing in your book. This can take several hours a week.

Most offices do keep one set of master books which an agent can refer to as a checkpoint. Human nature being what it is, however, these are not always up to date, and they are not available at all when you are making phone calls from your home in the evening. Just about everyone agrees that nothing can replace an agent's own accurately kept set of books. Some agents are more conscientious about this than others, but all agree it is one of the job's headaches.

Besides keeping up with the market, there is often other paperwork involved in being a real estate agent. Especially in smaller offices (and most real estate agencies are still small businesses), an agent is required to make a file folder for each new property that she lists. She must also fill out and send the property description to the Multiple Listing Service; write some sample newspaper advertisements for it; type notices of any changes in price or terms; notify the board of a deposit taken; make copies of contracts for banks and/or lawyers; help fill out and often distribute mortgage applications; and generally keep all parties concerned posted on what is happening as the deal approaches its closing date. To this add the work of keeping files on old customers and new leads, canvassing records, and of course time schedules and appointment calendars.

Some of the largest firms in the country have clerical staffs and special mortgage and closing departments to follow through on some of these jobs and thus free the agent's time for agenting.

MEETINGS

The time that large real estate firms save their agents by minimizing clerical work is often devoured by meetings. It seems the larger the firm the more frequent and varied the meetings. Sales meetings, listing meetings, policy meetings, and just plain office meetings. Sometimes they are tightly controlled and time-limited by the chairperson, sometimes they get into circular arguments which last for hours.

Generally meetings are few in small firms. A broker with three agents working in the office can talk with and sample the opinions of each individually. Most policy decisions are then made by that broker alone. It may sound autocratic, but it does save hours.

QUALIFYING

Qualifying buyers actually takes little time, but it runs a close second to canvassing as the job most frequently skipped by agents. The reason? It's unpleasant and sometimes awkward.

To qualify a buying couple, an agent must ask them how much money they make, how much they have managed to save for a down payment, and the names of their banks and credit and employment references. These are very personal questions and many agents have a difficult time asking them. As a result, they often take out unqualified couples and often waste a good deal of time showing them houses they cannot possibly afford before getting down to the business of talking about income and payments.

Some more efficient offices have circumvented this problem with a home-buying questionnaire to be filled out during the first meeting with the agent. It asks all the qualification questions along with others which give a profile of family lifestyle and needs and wants in a house. And many people are more willing to fill out a form about their financial status than they are to answer direct oral questions asked by an agent. The written form also has the advantage of being a permanent record from which the agent can work.

NEGOTIATING

This is headache time, floor-pacing time, opening-the-refrigerator-door time, smoking time, drinking time, blowing-up-at-your-spouse-and-kids time, slamming-doors time. Whatever it is that you tend to do under stress, this is the time for it. When negotiating, a real estate agent is a mediator, but a mediator with a personal stake in the game—her commission. She cannot help getting involved in the emotional tension that peaks for both buyers and sellers when offers are made and the bargaining gets serious.

Sometimes the negotiating is relatively simple—an offer, a counter offer, an acceptance, and signatures all around—perhaps an evening's work. Sometimes it goes on for days—occasionally even a week or more—and the tension can be excruciating. Often there are phone calls at every imaginable hour. Everyone wants the agent available the very instant they call and wants answers within the next half hour. And sometimes the deal falls apart, and all the work is for nothing.

FINANCING

Few people can buy a house today without a mortgage so helping with the financing has become an important job in every real estate office. Again some of our giant firms have mortgage or financing departments to which a prospective home buyer is transferred as soon as the ink is dry on the contracts. In the majority of firms, however, the selling agent is also a mortgage hunter.

Mortgage hunting might require several hours of phone calls, several visits to banks, and the filling out of a dozen or so forms. The work can sometimes be made a little easier by keeping a well-stocked file of mortgage applications from all area lenders in the office and by keeping in close touch with representatives from these lenders so that accurate profiles of their requirements are always available. But nothing replaces personal contact and firsthand knowledge, and a top agent devotes some time each week to keeping her finger on the pulse of the mortgage market.

ATTENDING CLOSINGS

No one gets paid in real estate until the house closes. The closing is the time and place when buyers and sellers and their lawyers or their closing agents sit down together, sign papers, and exchange cash (usually in the form of checks) and property deeds. It is also the time when the commission check is written to the real estate firm which sold the house.

Very few closings take more than an hour and a half and most selling agents gladly attend them. There are usually handshakes and thank yous all around (the problems have been solved or forgotten or you wouldn't be at the closing table) and the agent usually departs with a handsome check (to be divided into less handsome checks at the broker's desk).

EXTRAS

Working in real estate is many things, but it is almost never boring. The time frames of each day change and the pace is usually varied. After a short time in the business, an agent has a working acquaintance with a large number of people and there are always new people to meet. There are times that are almost frantic, and there are times to sit about comfortably and enjoy coffee and a chat with coworkers. There are professional organizations that an agent can join and to which she can devote a good deal or just a bit of time. And there is a certain amount of customer entertaining.

I don't mean to imply that real estate agents buy expensive theater tickets to Broadway shows or gala banquets for their customers; the entertaining is much more low key. Often showing houses to a good potential buyer will include a luncheon or two; or perhaps an evening's visit to the agent's home to talk about the area; or perhaps a day spent driving about getting to know area towns without ever going into a single house. Some agents also traditionally thank the people who send them referrals that materialize into sales with a luncheon or dinner date, and many agents give a housewarming gift to customers after they move into their new homes.

These extras are never constant in the course of any one week, but they are a part of the job. They demand time and sometimes money; they are also often fun.

Having written all this, it seems almost redundant to say that in today's residential real estate market being an agent takes a *lot* of time. Many people who start out thinking that they have found a part-time job find themselves spending *more* than forty hours a week on their work. It's *not* easy, but the career does offer the advantage that many of those hours are unfixed and can be scheduled to fit the individual agent's needs, and most often extra hours and extra effort are rewarded with extra income.

TWO

Are You the Type?

Is MY description of a real estate career a little intimidating? Perhaps you're thinking that only Superwoman (disguised as a composite of Lois Lane, Bo Derek, and Mom Walton) could do it all and still have time left over to shop occasionally for a new outfit; or put on her jeans and dig in the garden; or give her children a comfortable hug.

Not so. Remember all aspects of the job do not make equal demands on any given day or in any given week. There are slow days and slow seasons. The erratic hours, the keen competition, the tension, the disappointments, the excitement of success, and the self-discipline all do take a little getting used to, but there is a world in the residential marketplace that *can* be merged with wifehood, or motherhood, or singledom, or a second career in maturity while at the same time retaining not only your sanity but also your sense of humor and a little *joie de vivre.* And as a bonus, there's the money.

Is it for you? Are you the real estate type? I don't know; only you can answer that question. To do so, however, you need a standard to judge by, a profile of the real estate type, if there is such a thing.

Let me digress and indulge my fantasy for just a few moments to demonstrate to you why I added "if there is such a thing" to that last sentence. I've always been fascinated by the murals of Renaissance Italy, those wonderful people-filled walls with each person a carefully executed portrait. If you'll bear with me (and promise not to laugh), I'd like to paint a mini-mural in words of a luncheon meeting of women residential real estate agents.

Of course I'll want action and movement in the painting, so I'll choose to portray the moment when the luncheon and meeting have just ended, when people begin to move around, talk to each other, and get ready to leave. At a prominent place in the center of the composition is a woman dressed in a silver-blue tailored wool suit. Her hair is gray and perfectly, beautifully styled to frame her face. She wears some gold jewelry and plain black pumps, and she is smiling and shaking hands with another woman. You guess that she was the speaker for the luncheon and that she is refined, competent, and financially comfortable.

The handshaker is a somewhat younger woman, dark-haired, perhaps in her early fifties. She is dressed in an equally conservative but not quite as expensive wool dress with a scarf and a gold circle pin at the neck. There is a feeling of animation and energy in her pose. You guess that she is an officer of the group, proud of her position and successful in her job.

Three women have remained seated at a table near by. They are obviously involved in a spirited discussion. The one speaking is Black, her hair teased to a high Afro, her makeup impeccable, her clothes high-fashion and bright, her leather boots stylish, her finger nails long, painted, and well manicured.

On her left sits a woman in a burgundy polyester knit pant suit. She wears no jewelry except a wide diamond-chip-studded wedding band. Her brown hair is pulled back tightly to a French twist and she wears lipstick that is a little too red and spots of rouge a little too round on her cheeks. She is somewhat overweight, there is a spot of salad dressing on the lapel of her suit, she is holding a huge purse on her lap. It is obvious that she is anxious to speak her ideas as one hand is partly raised and open and her feet under her chair are resting only on the toes. Her shoes are in need of polish and the back of the right one is badly worn, obviously at the point where it rubs against the floor when she is driving customers about in the car.

The third chair at this table is occupied by a very thin, nervous-looking woman. Her skin is somewhat coarse, she wears no makeup, no jewelry, and is dressed in a peasant jumper and an old-fashioned style blouse. Her hair is naturally blond, fine, and although curled by a recent permanent, limp. Her nails are bitten and she wears a Band-aid on one finger. She is taking a cigarette from a half empty pack. The ash tray in front of her is full.

A little farther in the background and to the left stands a heavy, big-busted, strong-looking woman whose straight, stringy hair is held back from her face by a stretch hair band. She is waving her arm in the air as she talks, and you could easily imagine her in a portrait group of lady wrestlers. Her dress is unbelted, straight, and plain. Her stockings have a run.

She is talking to, and intimidating, a diminutive Hispanic woman in her late thirties. This small woman's dark eyes look intently up at the speaker. Her long, smooth, shining black hair is clasped at the back of her neck by a simple hand-carved wooden barrette. Her clothes are a neat but rather ordinary skirt and sweater. You guess from her appearance and attitude that she is serious, attentive, quiet, and efficient, and for some inexplicable reason you also guess that she is kind.

On the other side of the painting, in the space to the right of and behind the central well-groomed pair, three young women stand talking together. Each is attractive and well-dressed, although the style of their clothing ranges from high-fashion, to conservative, to Simplicity's designer patterns for home sewing. One of these women is writing in a small notebook, the other two are exchanging business cards. They have a sense of professionalism about them, a sense of determination to succeed.

Farther to the right, a somewhat angular middle-aged woman gathers the matchbooks left on the table and slips them into her purse. Her outfit is neat, but obviously discount department store, her shoes are too shiny to be leather. She is a middle person, middle brown hair, middle colored skin, middle height, middle weight, the kind of person who would go unnoticed among the housewives in a supermarket or the patients waiting in a dentist's office.

Nearby a plump, motherly looking redhead is pulling on her coat and glancing at her watch at the same time. You guess that you see in her face a concern that she won't be home in time to meet the school bus. There are mud stains on the hem of her coat, and on the table near her is a napkin full of leftover dessert cookies that she has gathered to take with her as a treat for her children.

In the background of the painting, four women relax near the bar. Their conversation is obviously casual, social. Two are middle-aged, carefully dressed, well mannered, professional looking. Another is quite old, perhaps in her seventies, but thin, energetic, and bright. Her animated conversation is directed toward a very young woman in jeans and boots and a bulky sweater. The young woman is shaking her head, swinging the heavy braid which falls almost to her waist, but her face is alight with delight and enthusiasm.

Well, which of the ladies in my mini-mural is "the real estate type"? Hardly a question, is it? Of course you knew when I began painting that I was leading you to the answer: "There is no type." Residential real estate sales is a profession which attracts an extremely wide spectrum of people. Women enter it who have middle-income husbands and families ranging in age from toddlers, to collegiates, or grandchildren. Women enter it who are single, or just married, or just divorced, or just ready to go back to work after the children are grown. Some need the income badly; others want the extras that their commissions can buy; others are financially comfortable but enjoy the stimulation of working; others are ambitious; others are socially competitive and materialistic. They are tall and short, fat and skinny, beautiful and plain, Black and white, quiet and vivacious, careful and casual, and young and old. And none of it matters. Any of these women can be a successful residential agent.

So what does it take, really? Am I saying that *everyone* is the real estate type? No. Some qualities and characteristics *are* prevalent among the vast majority of successful agents, but they are not qualities easily identified on first impression. They are not socioeconomic standards or physical features. The profile of the real estate type against which you may want to measure yourself is a profile of intangible personal characteristics.

And yes, I do have a list for you. It is a list which grew first from my own observations and was then verified by my readings of research studies on women in the business world. Those research studies gave me a sense of confidence that the profile I was drawing for you was a valid one. The comments I have made on the items in the list, however, are entirely my own.

On a scale of one to ten (ten being the highest) no one could possibly rate a ten in each category of this list. (Or if someone did, I don't think I'd want to know her. Too much goodness makes me *very* uncomfortable.) But most successful agents will rank five or better on each of the following. This doesn't mean that you can't see yourself as a two right now and set your sights on getting to a seven later. The list is merely a guideline to help you look at yourself in terms of what it takes to make it in this job *before* you commit yourself to several months of work and red tape.

AGGRESSIVE, ASSERTIVE, COMPETITIVE

One broker for whom I worked thought he was paying me a compliment when he introduced me to his wife saying, "Carolyn is my most aggressive salesman." I didn't like it. I didn't like being called a sales*man* and I was offended by being described as aggressive.

Aggressive in my mind had to do with fighting, pushing, and grabbing, and I had never pictured myself in that way. Yes, I went after listings. Yes, I worked hard on sales. But I played by the rules and I honestly tried *not* to step on other people along the way. Why did he see me as aggressive?

The word bothered me so much that I mentioned it to my husband at dinner that night. "You have the wrong meaning," he said. "Its connotation is entirely different in the business world."

I didn't believe him and took refuge in my dictionary. But it turned out that that dictionary sided with the men. Definition # 1: "disposed to attack or encroach." Aha, I thought, I knew it! And then definition # 2: "self-assertive; also enterprising; as an aggressive sales manager."

Yes, I admitted to myself, I was self-assertive and enterprising. And if that's what aggressive really meant, I guessed that I was indeed an aggressive salesperson. But I still balked. I wanted to draw a very *firm* line between that definition and "disposed to attack or encroach."

Salespeople, especially used car and real estate salespeople, have something of a bad image in this country. Include "real estate sales agent" in one of those connotation games where you go through a list of words like cat, love, home, etc. and the respondent says "dog," "hate," "mother," or whatever else pops into his or her mind and you'll probably get responses like "pushy," "high pressure," "cover-ups," "dog-eat-dog," or "you got me, I can't think of a thing!" I've never heard anyone say "loyal," "hard working," "dedicated," "honest," "sincere"—I'd better stop, I think I'm carrying this too far.

But image aside, what is it really like out there trying to beat out the competition and make a living too? Can you succeed in this business if you don't see yourself as aggressive, meaning that you won't attack a prey or encroach upon the work of another agent? My answer is an unqualified *yes.*

There may be (in fact there usually is) a bad apple in every barrel, but most sales agents are neither warlike nor unscrupulous, and you can usually spot the few who are quite early in the game and give them a wide breadth or deal with them defensively. What you do need in this game is an aggressive attitude, aggressive meaning self-assertive and self-starting.

Back to my well-worn desk dictionary. *Assertive*: "disposed to assertion, positive" and *assert*: "to state positively, affirm, aver." No one can survive in the residential marketplace without a positive belief in her position, her rights, and her opinions. Assertiveness is an absolute essential. Without it a woman agent will become an errand girl, at the beck and call of every customer and every broker for whom she works.

But to stand up positively without being warlike is one thing; to take steps forward and then finally to run in the race is yet another. Now we are talking about the competitive spirit, and there's no way around it, a top agent is competitive. She goes after listings and sales hoping and planning to win, giving it her best try, and knowing that sometimes she will win and sometimes she will lose.

Some agents are more competitive and enjoy the race more than others, but everyone who survives in the business has some degree of the competitive spirit. But remember competitiveness does *not* rule out a sense of ethics and a respect for one's fellow beings. In fact, I would bet the correlation is positive: most often competitiveness and respect go hand in hand.

SELF-RELIANT AND SELF-CONFIDENT

The woman who wants to be assigned one chore at a time along with specific directions as to how to complete that chore, with periodic checks by a supervisor, and finally with an "Atta girl" at the end of the job has no place in the residential real estate game. In this job, you are on your own most of the time. No boss hovers around telling you how to answer or ask questions; which listings to pick out to show a customer; how to plan the best route for the showings; what to do if you get a flat tire; how to calm angry sellers during negotiation; or how to find your way out of the maze of streets and dead ends when you're lost in a giant development. You have to be the kind of woman who once got pluses in the grade-school report-card space labeled "self-reliance."

Many people would probably also guess that the ideal woman agent was once the little sixth grader whose teacher told her parents, "She has tremendous leadership potential." I'm not sure, however, that that guess would be a good one. Certainly the ideal woman agent is *not* a follower, but those pearls of teacher praise, "leadership potential," are not really synonymous with self-reliance. A good agent doesn't need the inborn impulse to pick up the flag and say "Follow me, guys!" Self-reliance is much more closely aligned to self-confidence. And self-confidence is a factor of success in almost every human endeavor.

It makes little difference whether you are about to make a difficult leap in a figure-skating competition, or in playing a Beethoven piano sonata, or into the question "Would you like to make an offer on this house?"; in order to succeed, you must *believe* that you can do it. If you stop to think and worry about your ability to accomplish the task, the odds are you will fail. And that's the way it is every day with every decision and problem in the real estate business—you must *believe* that you can handle it and then proceed with the best of your ability. Sometimes you may fall, sometimes you may hit a wrong note, and sometimes you may get a negative response, but more and more often, as your ability and skill increase, you will succeed. To rely on yourself and believe in yourself is to discover new strengths and to give yourself the opportunity to grow.

ACTIVE

This century began with a Victorian image of womanhood. If I were to characterize that image in a word, it would be "passive." Women were depicted, and seen, and saw themselves as "receivers." Things were done to them and for them. The woman's movement from the suffragettes to the ERA has been a fight against this attitude, against linking "feminine" with docile, submissive, weak, subservient, sweet, obedient, compliant, yielding, and *passive.*

Today the Victorian mold is being broken, perhaps more slowly than women activists would like, but definitely broken. And with the breaking of the mold, career opportunities for women have been opening up in fields that demand an active attitude toward work. The selling of residential real estate was one of the first of these careers.

No agent can be docile, submissive, subservient, and passive and succeed in this business. That is not to say that a woman need carry a big stick, walk tall, and smoke a cigar, but only that she must be willing to initiate activity, set goals for herself, approach and activate other people, and step forward unafraid.

RISK-TAKING AND CREATIVE

There's an adage among real estate agents across the country: "Buyers are liars!" "That's not nice," you say. I agree, but it's true. Sometimes the truth of the adage is demonstrated because people deliberately falsify financial information, but much more often its truth is demonstrated in buyer ignorance. Very often buyers are liars because they simply don't *know* what they *really* want in a house.

Everyone has heard the story about the couple who told every agent they went out with that they would look at split-levels only. They looked at split-levels for six months with at least eight different agents. Nothing pleased them until one day a risk-taking agent drove them up to a ranch, which they promptly bought.

That agent showed creativity and made the sale. I know, you're thinking, "So what's the risk?" Her very real risk was in losing those customers. Unlike a listing client who signs up with an agency for a specified period of time, buyers can leave an agent at the drop of a hat or can work with several different agents at the same time. When an agent deviates from the directions given her, she risks dissatisfaction and anger.

I don't mean to imply that a good agent disregards the directives and specifications of her customers, but only that she is occasionally willing to try the unconventional and/or the unexpected approach to a situation. This *is* risk-taking, for leaving the conventional path increases her chances of losing along with her chances of winning. But everyone who wants to win must be willing to risk falling off the painted horse for a chance at the brass ring.

Top agents are willing to show a special contemporary to customers who insist they want a colonial, or to present seriously an offer $20,000 *under* the asking price, or to take the listing on a house even a kind ad man would call a "handy-man special." Risk-taking success is a frame of mind that says, "Well . . . maybe, *maybe* there's a chance." It's a frame of mind that can see a new angle, a view from a different perspective.

This kind of risk-taking is deeply embedded in human creativity. In his book, *The Courage To Create* (W.W. Norton & Co., 1975) Rollo May says of creative people, "They knock on silence for an answering music." I would add, though the addition is less poetic, that they also look to see what is not yet there.

The risk-taking, creative agent is not afraid to show the dirty, cluttered house that is structurally sound even if her customer is a junior executive with a white-glove wife. She is quick to point out that in an older house a family room could easily be added behind the kitchen, especially if the house is otherwise perfect for the family-of-seven customers she is taking out. She doesn't take "no" for an answer when negotiating until she has explored every possible compromise. She doesn't take "no" for an answer from the mortgage company until she has explored every possible source of money. And she is very slow to believe that *any* situation is impossible.

To knock on silence is sometimes to risk playing the fool, but when there is an answer and that answer is music . . .

DECISIVE

Some real estate agents waste a good deal of desk time poring over six different listings trying to decide which four houses to show in the available time. And worse yet, some can't make the decision and try to squeeze in all six.

If you're the kind of person who stands in a crowded grocery aisle causing a minor carriage jam because you can't decide which brand of tuna to buy this week, or if you try on the same three dresses three times each and then put them all back on the rack and go to another store to try on three more dresses only to return to try on the original three again, or if you ask your husband or your best friend which evening school course you should take next semester, you will have difficulty in a real estate career, especially at the beginning.

Being a real estate agent involves making scores of decisions every day. They range in importance from which way to turn at an intersection when all you have is a house number to go by; to when to make a follow-up phone call; to which bank or lawyer to recommend; to (most important, touchy, and subtle of all) how to present offers and counter offers. Often an agent's outward appearance of assurance and positive commitment is a non-verbal message to the customer or client. It can sway him or her toward a decision more quickly than hours of verbal urging. An agent's vacillation and indecisiveness, on the other hand, can mean a missed opportunity and/or a lost customer.

Acting positively and decisively involves the ability to perceive alternatives quickly, evaluate them, and then choose among them. This skill is an inborn trait in some people, but for many others it must and can be learned and practiced.

ENERGETIC

Several years ago I read a magazine article about working as a real estate agent. It was written by a professional writer who followed a top sales agent about for a week or so. Somehow the word "energetic" in my outline triggered the memory of that article and I dug it out of the file. Sure enough, I found what I was looking for.

The article described a woman agent who jumped out of bed by 6:15 every weekday morning and called out reveille to her three children. She then trotted downstairs to empty the dishwasher as she prepared a full-course health breakfast for her husband, who left at seven for work, and for her children, who left at eight for school. She probably then gathered fresh daisies from the garden to arrange artistically in a milk-glass vase on the breakfast table, but the article didn't say so. It did say that she went on a daily race through the house, cleaning, picking up, sponging off, etc., before taking her shower, dressing, and leaving home by 10 minutes before 9. The article also didn't say so, but I would bet that this lady was dressed, coiffed, and made-up in the manner of a Washington diplomatic hostess *and* that she entered her office with a bright smile and a cheery good morning for everyone. She probably also jogs five miles a day, swims twice a week, and bakes her own bread, right?

No, I've never known an agent like this "typical profile." Most of us need coffee to get going in the morning, most of us fight midafternoon slump, and most of us hate working at night. So what do I mean by energetic? I mean the kind of individual who doesn't need to be *told* which chores need to be done or in what order, the kind of individual who can find the energy in herself to get up and get started.

My husband, who works for a large corporation, says there's an acronym for it, KYITA, pronounced kee-ta. If you'll pardon the language, the term expresses my meaning exactly. KYITA stands for Kick Yourself in the Ass. In real estate you must KYITA to get going a dozen times a day.

CANDID AND TACTFUL

How can anyone be both candid and tactful? Doesn't one trait negate the other? No, and in real estate both are equally important.

Because I live in a community near the headquarters of a major U. S. corporation that routinely transfers employees after three to five years in any one location, I've had the opportunity to listen to people talk about their experiences with real estate agents while remaining an anonymous member of the social gathering. It has been interesting and enlightening. I could literally fill this book with their stories, but I would rather share with you a bit of praise.

The most appreciated, most often discussed quality in a real estate agent is *honesty.* I don't mean the "not stealing" kind of honesty, I mean the willingness to share her honest evaluation of the faults and virtues of a piece of property. The agent who most often gets referrals is the one who will candidly tell her customers that "this house looks as though it sometimes gets water in the basement" or "I agree those woods behind the property are beautiful, but there are plans for a highway to cut through there sometime in the next three years." This kind of candid sharing of her special knowledge may turn a house-buying couple off on a particular house that they think they are in love with, but it will usually strengthen their loyalty to the agent who told them about the problem.

Where does tact come in? Imagine yourself taking a listing. The house is structurally sound and in a good neighborhood, but it has been lived in hard by a family consisting of four young children and two parents who would rather sculpt clay models of the Sesame Street muppets than snoop around with a spray bottle of Mr. Clean and a sponge every day. How do you tell those parents that their house will sell more quickly and for more money if they do some painting, wash the walls, windows, and banisters, keep the dirty clothes from overflowing the hampers, get the crunchies and stickies off the kitchen floor, put the cat litter box in the garage, allow for standing room for three people among the toys in each child's bedroom, put the ironing board away, and brush the dog hair off the couch? It takes tact.

INTELLIGENT AND RESPONSIBLE

You don't need an I.Q. of 140 or a college degree to be successful in the real estate world. You do need perceptive insight into people and situations, and the ability to listen, see, read, and make your own evaluations. You need to know instinctively when to be quiet and when to speak up. You need to be able to operate a pocket calculator and read mortgage interest rate books and legal contracts. But you do *not* need to be able to write the contracts or advise on them; that's a lawyer's job. You need to understand square footage and mill rates, and you need to know what's going on in the world, the country, and especially the towns in which you work.

The job requires what most people would call "good common sense," but it also requires that you take common sense one step further to responsibility. You must be willing to get done what you say you will get done, in the time you say you will get it done. You must respect the privacy and property of your customers and clients. And to survive in the job, you *must not forget* about your responsibility to your family and yourself.

AT EASE WITH OTHER PEOPLE

If a random group of one hundred people were asked "What is the personality trait most essential in a salesperson?", I would guess that the number one answer would be: "at ease with other people." And I would wonder exactly what "at ease with other people" meant to the people who chose that answer. Were they thinking of back-slapping, joke-telling, one-of-the-guys type salespeople? Were they thinking of dominance and directiveness? Or the stereotype of the gregarious extrovert? Or acquiescence? Or the ability to make small talk?

To me being at ease with other people *is* one of the most essential ingredients of success, but it is none of the characteristics I have just mentioned or of a hundred other traits either. It is simply being yourself, being yourself without masks or pretense. When you can be yourself proudly, you are automatically at ease with other people.

Which leads me to a kind of summary. Every one of the character traits in this list is important in this game, but above all else *being yourself,* being secure in your self-worth and having a realistic knowledge of your strengths and weaknesses, is the most important single element in achieving success as a woman in residential real estate. Or for that matter in any career and on every day.

THREE

The License

IT WAS the first night of my first real estate licensing course. The instructor stomped in five minutes late and deposited his armload of books, folders, and papers on the lectern with the thud of a heavy gavel. There was an immediate silence, but he stepped out from behind the authoritative barricade anyway, came forward, and stood toe to toe with the person sitting in the center seat of the front row. He put his hands on his hips, bent slightly forward for effect, glared at us, and boomed, "Do you know why you're here?"

Forty people stopped breathing. I would have sworn he stood there motionless and menacing for a full sixty seconds, but it was probably ten. "You're here," he continued, lowering his voice to a cordial growl, "you're here because this state can't *afford* to let you loose out there untrained." He turned his back and returned to the lectern.

I looked around the room. About 70 percent of the class was made up of women ranging in age from late youth to late maturity. For the most part, the men in the group were either younger or older, but they seemed quite ordinary. Not one person bore the slightest resemblance to a ferocious beast which might wreak havoc upon the neighboring communities if "let loose untrained."

So why the fuss? Why were we there anyway? Not for any idealistic quest for knowledge, I assure you, or even for training. We were there because the course was required by the state before a candidate could take the real estate salesperson's license exam. We were there to learn what the state insisted we know before we were "let loose."

I think I wanted that New Jersey license as much as anyone in that room, but I think I felt more resentment than most of the other students toward the instructor's antagonistic attitude, and later, as weekly sessions passed, toward the boredom of counting ceiling tiles and trucks passing on the highway outside the window.

At that time New Jersey would neither honor my Connecticut license nor acknowledge my two years of working experience. I had been sent back to square one in the game and I didn't like it. I learned later, however, that mine was a common problem among agents who apply for a license in another state, and an especially common problem among women agents who happen to be married to corporate middle-management men and who therefore are routinely moved about the country.

There is no standard procedure for getting a real estate license in this country. Each state is autonomous in enacting and enforcing its real estate laws, and the autonomy is nowhere more evident than in licensing law requirements. After the first license law was passed in California in 1917, the idea of requirements, procedures, and regulations spread across the country with the speed of breeding rabbits. Today the only universally valid statements that can be made about real estate licensing laws are that every state requires a license to sell real estate, every state administers a licensing examination, and every state differentiates between a broker's license and a salesperson's license.

Throughout the country, the broker's license is actually the only valid license to conduct real estate business. Only a broker can enter into a contract to act as an agent for either seller or buyer, and only a broker can establish a fiduciary (trust) relationship to handle, hold, or transfer deposit monies. Translated into workaday activities, these restrictions mean that only a broker can take a listing, advertise, and sell a house.

"So what is a salesperson?" you justifiably ask. A salesperson is essentially a stand-in for a broker. A salesperson takes listings and sells houses *for* the broker by whom she is employed. The broker may never set foot into the house being listed, but it is the *broker's* listing and either the broker or an officer of the brokerage corporation must sign the listing contract. If a salesperson leaves the employ of a broker, all of the unsold listings that she has brought into the office remain with the broker, as do all sales pending. I'll get into these procedures in more detail in Chapter 10, but for now keep in mind that, in theory at least, the salesperson is not allowed to transact any business without the knowledge, supervision, and consent of her employing broker.

"Why not be a broker then?" is of course your next question. And I answer, "Yes, the position is better, but it's not quite as easy as just *deciding* to be a broker." Most states now require that every aspiring broker work for a period of time as a salesperson before applying for a broker's license, and even the few states that allow candidates to take the broker's examination without work experience have more stringent requirements for that examination.

The vast majority of people in real estate therefore start their careers as sales agents. Because of this fact and because this book is written for *beginning* agents, I have limited the information in the following survey of licensing requirements throughout the United States to data pertinent to the salesperson's license. I have included, however, the length of the apprenticeship required in each state for a broker's license and the specific requirements for that license in the states without an apprenticeship period. I have also indicated residency requirements for licensing in each state and named the states where reciprocity agreements may allow an experienced agent to bypass some or all of the pre-licensing requirements and procedures.

In discussing the requirements for actually making application, I mention "recovery fund amounts" and "bond amounts." Both monetary holdings are a means of protecting the state and its real estate agents against complaints, claims, and litigation. In states where a bond must be posted, the salesperson purchases the bond from an insurance company. The cost is dependent on the amount of the bond required, but it is usually fairly small. In states which maintain a recovery fund, each licensee is assessed a dollar figure, again usually a relatively small amount, in order to maintain the total dollar figure set by the state as the recovery fund. Some of these state assessments are a one-time fee; others are included in the cost of the original license and renewals; still others fluctuate from time to time.

Regarding the licensing examinations themselves, many states are now using standardized tests. These are most often provided by one of the two largest testing agencies in this country—the Educational Testing Service and the American College of Testing, and I will indicate the source of the test being used in each state by the abbreviations ETS or ACT. This designation does not mean, however, that the same test is given in two different states. There is a Uniform Licensing Examination used extensively, but both services also tailor portions of their exams to fit the specific real estate laws of the state in which they are given. When a state designs and administers its own test, I will indicate "staff" or "commission" as the source of the exam.

The following state-by-state profiles have been compiled from my personal survey of real estate licensing administrators across the country and from the 1981 report of the National Association of Real Estate License Law Officials. Like everything else in this late twentieth-century world, however, all the information is subject to change (especially the fees). Use it therefore as a guideline, but check for changes with the real estate administrative officials of your state (addresses are included) when you are ready to apply for your particular license.

ALABAMA

Real Estate Commission
State Capitol
750 Washington Avenue
Montgomery, Alabama 36130

Education requirements. Proof of high school graduation or the equivalent thereof; and 45 clock hours in pre-license real estate course work taught over a minimum period of eight weeks.

Application requirements. Photograph; $25,000 bond; and a sworn statement by the broker under whom the applicant desires to be licensed certifying that in his opinion the applicant is honest, trustworthy, of good reputation, and recommending that the license be granted to the applicant and accepting responsibility for the actions of such salesperson.

Examination information. ACT exam given in 10 sessions per year. The exam writing time is 3 hours. No limit on retakes. Calculators permitted.

Fees. Exam fee $50; re-exam fee $50. Original license $15; renewal license $15 each year.

Continuing education requirements. None.

Residency requirement. Ninety days.

Reciprocity. None.

Publications. License law booklet.

Experience requirements for a broker's license. Two years experience as a salesperson or 15 college semester hours in real estate subjects.

ALASKA Department of Commerce & Economic Development
Real Estate Commission
142 East Third Avenue
Anchorage, Alaska 99501

Education requirements. None.

Application requirements. Photograph; and $50,000 recovery fund coverage for which the assessment fee is $40 for two years.

Examination information. ETS exam given in 11 sessions per year. The exam writing time is 4½ hours. No limit on retakes. Calculators permitted.

Fees. Exam fee $50; re-exam fee $50. Original license $50; renewal license $50 for two years.

Continuing education requirements: None.

Residency requirements: Ninety days.

Reciprocity. None, but out-of-state licenses are available under certain conditions.

Publications. Alaska Statutes and Regulations Relating to Real Estate Brokers and Salesmen; Alaska real estate study manual is available.

Experience requirement for a broker's license. Twenty-four months continuous active work as a licensed salesperson.

ARIZONA Department of Real Estate
1645 West Jefferson
Phoenix, Arizona 85007

Education requirements. 45 classroom hours of instruction approved by the Arizona Real Estate Commission.

Application requirements. Photograph; fingerprints; affidavit of completion of education requirement; and $20,000 recovery fund coverage for which there is a $10 one-time-only fee.

Examination information. Staff or Commission exam given in 12 sessions per year. The exam writing time is 3¼ hours. No limit on retakes. Calculators permitted.

Fees. Exam fee $25; re-exam fee $25. Original license $50; renewal license $50 for each two years.

Continuing education requirements. 12 hours of classroom study in real estate subjects approved by the Commission.

Residency requirement. Ninety days.

Reciprocity. None.

Publications. Instructions to License Applicants; Arizona License Law ($1.00); Directory of Licensed Real Estate Salespeople and Brokers ($2.00); regular newsletter.

Experience requirements for a broker's license. Three years as a salesperson during the five years immediately preceding the time of application for the broker's license and 90 additional hours of classroom study.

ARKANSAS Real Estate Commission
#1 Riverfront Place, Suite 660
North Little Rock, Arkansas 72114

Education requirements. None.

Application requirements. Photograph; credit report; $25 recovery fund fee; and written recommendation of five local citizens who have owned real estate for a period of five years or more.

Examination information. ETS exam given in 11 sessions per year. The exam writing time is 4 hours. No limit on retakes. Calculators permitted.

Fees. Exam fee $15; re-exam fee $15. Original license $10; renewal license $10 for two years.

Continuing education requirements. 30 clock hours in principles of real estate within 12 months after passing the examination.

Residency requirement. None.

Reciprocity. Partial with Connecticut, District of Columbia, Illinois, Indiana, Kansas, Louisiana, Missouri, Nebraska, New Jersey, New York, North Carolina, Oklahoma, Tennessee.

Publications. Real Estate License Law and Regulations.

Experience requirements for a broker's license. Active experience as a real estate salesperson for twenty-four of the last forty-eight months in Arkansas or any other state and 30 classroom hours or 3 college semester hours study in real estate. Or 90 classroom hours or 6 college semester hours study in real estate without working experience.

CALIFORNIA Real Estate Commission
Post Office Box 160009
Sacramento, California 95816

Education requirements. None.

Application requirements. Fingerprints and $100,000 recovery fund coverage included in the license fee.

Examination information. Staff exam given in numerous sessions. The exam writing time is 3¼ hours. No limit on retakes. Calculators permitted.

Fees. Exam fee $10; re-exam fee $10. Original license $45 for four years; renewal license $45 for four years.

Continuing education requirements. For active renewals, 45 clock hours of classroom study for each renewal period.

Residency requirement. None.

Reciprocity. None.

Publications. State real estate study manual; regular newsletter; other periodical publications.

Experience requirements for a broker's license. Two years full-time sales experience or a BA degree.

COLORADO Real Estate Commission
110 State Services Building
1525 Sherman Street
Denver, Colorado 80203

Education requirements. 48 classroom hours of real estate principles and real estate law.

Application requirements. Fingerprints; $50,000 recovery fund coverage; and recommendation of broker by whom the applicant will be employed.

Examination information. ETS exam given in 11 sessions per year. The exam writing time is 4½ hours. No limit on retakes. Calculators permitted.

Fees. Exam fee $13.25; re-exam fee $13.25. Original license $28 for current year only; renewal license $33 for three years.

Continuing education requirements. None.

Residency requirement. None.

Reciprocity. Partial with states that give the multi-state portion of the license exam separate from the local portion.

Publications. State real estate study manual; regular newsletter; license law pamphlet.

Experience requirements for a broker's license. Two years active work as a salesperson in Colorado or the experience equivalent.

CONNECTICUT

Real Estate Commission
90 Washington Street
Hartford, Connecticut 06115

Education requirements. 30 classroom hours in principles of real estate.

Application requirements. Recovery fund coverage of $10,000 for which there is a one-time fee of $20.

Examination information. University of Connecticut exam given in 60 sessions per year. The exam writing time is 4 hours. Two retake exams are permitted per year. Calculators permitted.

Fees. Exam fee $10; no fee for re-exam. Original license $75; renewal license $75 each year.

Continuing education requirements. None.

Residency requirement. None.

Reciprocity. Arkansas, Delaware, District of Columbia, Georgia, Massachusetts, New Jersey, Oklahoma, Rhode Island, Utah.

Publications. Licensing Laws & Regulations.

Experience requirements for a broker's license. Two years as a licensed salesperson.

DELAWARE — Real Estate Commission
Box 1401, Margaret O'Neill Building
Dover, Delaware 19901

Education requirements. 75 classroom hours in real estate study.

Application requirements. Recovery fund coverage of $10,000 for which there is a $25 one-time-only fee.

Examination information. ETS exam given in 12 sessions per year. The exam writing time is 4½ hours. Three retake exams are permitted per year. Calculators permitted.

Fees. Exam fee $15; re-exam fee $15. Original license $10; renewal license $10 each year.

Continuing education requirements. None.

Residency requirement. None.

Reciprocity. Connecticut, District of Columbia, Maryland, New Jersey, New York, North Carolina, Pennsylvania, Virginia.

Publications. Delaware Real Estate Primer (license laws).

Experience requirement for a broker's license. Five years active work as a licensed salesperson and the conclusion of at least thirty sales.

DISTRICT OF COLUMBIA — Real Estate Commission
Room 109
614 "H" Street, N.W.
Washington, D.C. 20001

Education requirements. None.

Application requirements. Credit report; $1,000 bond; name and business address of the real estate broker by whom the applicant is to be employed, and a written statement by that broker that the applicant, in his opinion, is honest, truthful, and of good reputation, and recommending that the license be granted to the applicant; and the recommendation of at least two residents of the District of Columbia, real estate owners, who owned real estate in the District of Columbia for a period of at least one year and who are not related to the applicant but who have personally known the applicant for a period of at least six months prior to the date of application, which recommendation shall certify that the applicant bears a good reputation for honesty, truthfulness, fair dealing, and competency, and recommend that a license be granted to the applicant.

Examination information. ETS exam given in 12 sessions per year. The exam writing time is 4 hours. Retakes are limited to twice within six months. Calculators permitted.

Fees. Exam fee $13; re-exam fee $13. Original license $50; renewal license $25 for each year.

Continuing education requirements. None.

Residency requirement. None.

Reciprocity. No full reciprocity; partial reciprocity under some circumstances.

Publications. District of Columbia real estate study manual is available.

Experience requirements for a broker's license. None.

FLORIDA

Real Estate Commission
Department of Professional &
Occupational Regulation
400 West Robinson Street
Orlando, Florida 32801

Education requirements. 51 classroom hours in real estate study approved by the Board of Real Estate.

Application requirements. Photograph and fingerprints.

Examination information. Staff or Commission exam given in 48 sessions per year. The exam writing time is 3½ hours. No limit on retakes. Calculators permitted.

Fees. Exam fee $25; re-exam fee $25. Original license $25; renewal license $20 for each two years.

Continuing education requirements. 14 classroom hours in real estate study each two years.

Residency requirement. Residency and domicile required at time of licensing.

Reciprocity. None.

Publications. Florida state real estate study manual is available; regular newsletter.

Experience requirements for a broker's license. Twelve months as a licensed salesperson in Florida.

GEORGIA Real Estate Commission
40 Pryor Street, S. W.
Atlanta, Georgia 30303

Education requirements. High school graduation or certificate of equivalency; and 24 classroom hours in real estate study, or 5 college quarter hours (3 semester hours) in real estate study at an accredited college or university.

Application requirements. Photograph; and recovery fund coverage of $20,000 for which there is a $10 one-time-only fee.

Examination information. ACT exam given on 11 dates per year. The exam writing time is 3 hours. No limit on retakes. Calculators permitted.

Fees. Exam fee $25; re-exam fee $25. Original license $15; renewal license $15 each two years.

Continuing education requirements. 80 hours during the first two years as a licensed salesperson; after January 1, 1982, 6 hours per two years.

Residency requirement. Residency required at time of licensing.

Reciprocity. Partial reciprocity with states giving ACT or ETS exam. Non-resident licensure agreements with Arkansas, Connecticut, Delaware, District of Columbia, Kentucky, Massachusetts, Nebraska, New Jersey, North Carolina, Oklahoma, South Carolina, Tennessee, Washington, and West Virginia.

Publications. Georgia real estate study manual available; regular newsletter; annual report; other course manuals.

Experience required for a broker's license. Three years experience as a salesperson in Georgia or another state.

HAWAII

Professional & Vocational Licensing Division
Department of Regulatory Agencies
Real Estate Commission
P. O. Box 3469
Honolulu, Hawaii 96801

Education requirements. Completion of a Hawaii approved 30-hour pre-license salesperson course; or previously licensed in a state with similar education requirements; or graduate of an accredited law school; or graduate of an accredited college with major in real estate; or completion of at least 12 semester hours in real estate at an accredited college; or GRI (Graduate Realtor Institute) designation.

Application requirements. Photograph; and $40,000 recovery fund coverage for which there is a $50 one-time-only fee.

Examination information. ETS exam given on 3 dates per year. The exam writing time is 3½ hours. No limit on retakes. Calculators permitted.

Fees. Exam fee $25; re-exam fee $25. Original license $50; renewal license $50 for each two years.

Continuing education requirements. None.

Residency requirement. No duration, but must be legal resident.

Reciprocity. None.

Publications. Hawaii Real Estate License Law and Rules and Regulations ($1.25); and regular newsletter.

Experience requirements for a broker's license. Two years active experience in Hawaii. (May be waived at the discretion of the Real Estate Commission.)

IDAHO Real Estate Commission
State Capitol Building
Boise, Idaho 83720

Education requirements. 45 classroom hours in essentials of real estate; and high school graduation or equivalency.

Application requirements. Fingerprints; credit report; and $2,000 recovery fund coverage for which the assessment is $20 for two years.

Examination information. ACT exam given in 36 sessions per year. The exam writing time is 5 hours. Twelve retakes permitted per year. Calculators permitted.

Fees. Exam fee $25; re-exam fee $10; Original license $60; renewal license $60 for each two years.

Continuing education requirements. None.

Residency requirement. Must be a resident upon activating license.

Reciprocity. Montana, Oregon, Utah, Washington.

Publications. Idaho state real estate study manual is available; regular newsletter; other publications.

Experience requirements for a broker's license. Two years of active license experience or allied experience.

ILLINOIS
Real Estate Commission
Department of Registration & Education
55 East Jackson Blvd.—17th Floor
Chicago, Illinois 60604

Education requirements. 30 classroom hour real estate transactions course from an approved school.

Application requirements. Recommendation of employing broker; photograph; $25 application fee; and recovery fund coverage of $50,000 for which there is a $10 fee for two years.

Examination information. ACT exam given in 12 sessions per year. The exam writing time is 3½ hours. Retakes are permitted once a month. Calculators permitted.

Fees. Exam fee $11.25; re-exam fee $11.25. Original license $35; renewal license $10 for two years.

Continuing education requirements. None.

Residency requirement. None.

Reciprocity. None.

Publications. Brokers and Salesmen License Act.

Experience requirements for a broker's license. One year as a licensed salesperson; or Bachelor's degree with the equivalent of a minor in real estate; or a license to practice law in Illinois.

INDIANA
Real Estate Commission
1022 State Office Building
100 North Senate Avenue
Indianapolis, Indiana 46204

Education requirements. 8 semester hours in real estate at an accredited college, or 40 clock hours in an Indiana approved real estate school.

Application requirements. Name and address of the broker who will employ applicant. A sworn certification by that broker of his intent to maintain the association with the salesperson is required within 120 days after passing the exam.

Examination information. ETS exam is given in 6 sessions per year. The exam writing time is 4 hours. No limit on retakes. Calculators permitted.

Fees. Exam fee $50; re-exam fee $50. Original license $25; renewal license $25 for each two years.

Continuing education requirements. None.

Residency requirement. None.

Reciprocity. Kentucky.

Publications. Real estate license law pamphlet; Indiana real estate study manual is available.

Experience requirements for a broker's license. Two years active experience as a salesperson or two years related real estate experience.

IOWA Real Estate Commission
Executive Hills
1223 East Court
Des Moines, Iowa 50319

Education requirements. 30 classroom hours in real estate study.

Application requirements. Fingerprints; credit report; and written recommendation of employing broker.

Examination information. ETS exam given in 12 sessions per year. The exam writing time is 4½ hours. No limit on retakes. Calculators permitted.

Fees. Exam fee $11; re-exam fee $11. Original license $10; renewal license $10 for each year.

Continuing education requirements. 7 classroom hours annually.

Residency requirement. None.

Reciprocity. Minnesota, Missouri, Nebraska, North Dakota, South Dakota.

Publications. Iowa state real estate study manual is available; regular newsletter.

Experience requirements for a broker's license. One year as a licensed salesperson.

KANSAS Real Estate Commission
535 Kansas Avenue
Room 1212
Topeka, Kansas 66603

Education requirements. High school education or proof of equivalency.

Application requirements. Credit report; $50,000 recovery fund coverage for which an assessment can be made; and recommendation under oath of a broker certifying that in the opinion of that broker the applicant is honest, truthful, and of good reputation, and recommending that a license be granted.

Examination information. ETS exam given in 12 sessions per year. The exam writing time is 4½ hours. Twelve retakes are permitted per year. Calculators permitted.

Fees. Exam fee $13; re-exam fee $13. Original license $15; renewal license $12 for each year.

Continuing education requirements. 30 classroom hours study during the first year as a salesperson and 30 additional hours during the second year.

Residency requirement. None.

Reciprocity. Full with Missouri, Oklahoma, Nebraska. Partial with Arkansas.

Publications. Kansas Real Estate Brokers' License Law.

Experience requirements for a broker's license. Two years as a salesperson during the five years immediately preceding application. Experience may be in Kansas or any other state.

KENTUCKY
Real Estate Commission
100 East Liberty Street
Suite 204
Louisville, Kentucky 40202

Education requirements. High school diploma or equivalent; and 6 academic hours or equivalent clock hours (96) in approved real estate courses.

Application requirements. Photograph; credit report; name and address of the licensed broker by whom the applicant will be employed; and $10,000 recovery fund coverage for which there is a fee of $30 for the first year.

Examination information. ETS exam given in 6 sessions per year. The exam writing time is 4½ hours. Two retakes are permitted per year. Calculators permitted.

Fees. Exam fee $25; re-exam fee $25. Original license $10; renewal license $10 for each year. $20 recovery fund fee with each renewal.

Continuing education requirements. 30 classroom hours instruction during the first two years as a licensed salesperson.

Residency requirement. None.

Reciprocity. Full with North Carolina, Ohio, and Tennessee. Partial with Georgia, New Jersey, West Virginia, and Missouri.

Publications. A Kentucky state real estate study manual is available; regular newsletter; supplementary material.

Experience requirements for a broker's license. Two years, reduced to one if applicant has attained associate's degree in real estate or baccalaureate degree with a major in real estate.

LOUISIANA
Real Estate Commission
P.O. Box 14785
Capitol Station
Baton Rouge, Louisiana 70808

Education requirements. High school graduation or certificate of equivalency; and 50 classroom hours in a real estate course approved by the Commission.

Application requirements. Photograph; credit report; sworn statement that the applicant is aware of and understands the provisions of the Fair Housing Act of 1968; and $20,000 recovery fund coverage which is included in the license fee.

Examination information. ETS exam given in 12 sessions per year. The exam writing time is 4½ hours. No limit on retakes. Calculators permitted.

Fees. Exam fee $25; re-exam fee $25. Original license $86; renewal license $58 for each two years. Recovery fund fee may fluctuate according to the amount of funds needed to maintain state reserve.

Continuing education requirements. 15 additional classroom hours of approved instruction before first renewal of license.

Residency requirement. Must be a resident of Louisiana.

Reciprocity. With some states under specific conditions approved by the Louisiana Real Estate Commission.

Publications. Louisiana state real estate study manual is available; regular newsletter.

Experience requirements for a broker's license. Two years active work as a licensed salesperson.

MAINE Department of Business Regulation
Real Estate Commission
State House—Station #35
Augusta, Maine 04333

Education requirements. High school education or its equivalent approved by the Commission.

Application requirements. Photograph; sworn statement of the applicant's present address and former residences; notarized recommendations of at least three citizens who have owned real estate for a period of one year or more in the county in which the applicant resides and who have known the applicant for a period of at least six months immediately prior to the date of application.

Examination information. University of Southern Maine exam given in 6 sessions per year. The exam writing time is 4½ hours. One retake is permitted per year. Calculators permitted.

Fees. Exam fee $40; first retake no charge. Original license $40; renewal license $40 for each two years.

Continuing education requirements. 12 clock hours of real estate oriented educational programs during each two-year license period.

Residency requirement. Must be resident for Maine license. Non-resident licenses available under certain conditions specified by the Commission.

Reciprocity. None.

Publications. Roster of Licensees; regular newsletter; booklet on licensing laws and rules.

Experience requirements for a broker's license. One year full time as a licensed salesperson, or a 90-hour approved course of study in real estate.

MARYLAND

Real Estate Commission
One South Calvert Street
Room 600
Baltimore, Maryland 21202

Education requirements. 45 clock hour course approved by the Maryland Real Estate Commission or a college level course in real estate.

Application requirements. Credit report.

Examination information. ETS exam given in 12 sessions per year. The exam writing time is 4½ hours. Three retakes permitted per year. Calculators permitted.

Fees. Exam fee $13; re-exam fee $13. Original license $20; renewal license $20 for each two years. $20 one-time-only fee for Real Estate Guaranty Fund.

Continuing education requirements. 12 clock hours of instruction in real estate subject matter approved by the Commission within every other two-year license renewal period.

Residency requirement. Permanent residency required for Maryland license. Non-resident licenses available under certain conditions specified and approved by the Commission.

Reciprocity. Full with Delaware, Pennsylvania, North Carolina, and Virginia. Partial with District of Columbia.

Publications. Real estate laws booklet.

Experience requirements for a broker's license. Three years experience as a licensed salesperson.

MASSACHUSETTS

Board of Registration of Real Estate Brokers and Salesmen
100 Cambridge Street
Boston, Massachusetts
02202

Education requirements. 24 hours in real estate study.

Application requirements. All applications for licenses to act as real estate salesmen shall be accompanied by the recommendation of three reputable citizens, not related to the applicant, who reside in or have their place of business in the Commonwealth, which recommendation shall certify that the applicant bears a good reputation for honesty and fair dealing and shall recommend that a license be granted to the applicant.

Examination information. ETS exam given in 12 sessions per year. The exam writing time is 4½ hours. No limit on retakes. Calculators permitted.

Fees. Exam fee $8.00; no fee for re-exam. Original license $20.83; renewal license $30 for each two years.

Continuing education requirements. None.

Residency requirement. One year for a Massachusetts license, but the requirement may be waived. Non-resident licenses are available to all states.

Reciprocity. Connecticut, District of Columbia, Georgia, New Jersey, New York, Rhode Island, Virginia, West Virginia.

Publications. None.

Experience requirements for a broker's license. One year as a licensed salesperson.

MICHIGAN — Deputy Real Estate Commissioner
Department of Licensing & Regulation
Post Office Box 30018
Lansing, Michigan 48909

Education requirements. 30 clock hours in real estate instruction if first state exam is failed.

Application requirements. Photograph; sponsoring broker.

Examination information. ETS exam given in 12 sessions per year. The exam writing time is 5 hours. No limit on retakes. Calculators permitted.

Fees. Exam fee, none; re-exam fee, none. Original license $25; renewal license $15 for each year.

Continuing education requirements. None.

Residency requirement. None.

Reciprocity. None.

Publications. None.

Experience requirements for a broker's license. Three years as a licensed salesperson.

MINNESOTA
Real Estate Director
Real Estate Commission
500 Metro Square Building
St. Paul, Minnesota 55101

Education requirements. 30 hours in real estate study pre-license.

Application requirements. $20,000 recovery fund coverage for which there is a $40 one-time-only fee.

Examination information. ETS exam given in 12 sessions per year. The exam writing time is 4½ hours. No limit on retakes. Calculators permitted.

Fees. Exam fee $13; re-exam fee $13. Original license $25; renewal license $10 for each year.

Continuing education requirements. 60 hours study within the first year of licensure; 45 hours in real estate course work every three years thereafter.

Residency requirement. None.

Reciprocity. Iowa, Nebraska, North Dakota, South Dakota. Some credit for out of state education programs and ETS exam.

Publications. Regular newsletter.

Experience requirements for a broker's license. Minimum of two years actual experience as licensed salesperson or five years related experience.

MISSISSIPPI
Real Estate Commission
754 North President Street
Jackson, Mississippi 39202

Education requirements. 6 semester hour course in real estate at a college or university, or 30 hours of real estate education as approved by the Realtor Institute of the National Institute of Realtors.

Application requirements. 2 photographs; credit report; and sworn statement by the employing broker that, in his opinion, the applicant is honest and trustworthy, and recommending that the license be granted the applicant.

Examination information. Staff or Commission exam given in 11 sessions per year. The exam writing time is 4 hours. Six retakes are permitted. Calculators are *not* permitted.

Fees. Exam fee $30; re-exam no charge. Original license $55; renewal license $20 per year.

Continuing education requirements. It is the duty of the broker to instruct his salesmen in regard to the fundamentals of real estate practice and the ethics of the profession.

Residency requirement. Must be a resident.

Reciprocity. None.

Publications. Real Estate Brokers License Act, Rules and Regulations; Code of Ethics; regular newsletter; some supplementary materials.

Experience requirements for a broker's license. Licensed as an active real estate salesperson in the state of Mississippi for twelve months prior to making application for the broker's license.

MISSOURI

Missouri Real Estate Commission
Post Office Box 1339
Jefferson City, Missouri 65102

Education requirements. 40 classroom hours in real estate instruction.

Application requirements. Application fee $20; photograph; credit report; notarized signature on the application form.

Examination information. ETS exam given in 12 sessions per year. The exam writing time is 4½ hours. No limit on retakes. Calculators permitted.

Fees. Exam fee $11; re-exam fee $11. Original license $5; renewal license $5 for each year.

Continuing education requirements. None.

Residency requirement. None.

Reciprocity. Iowa, Nebraska, Kansas, Oklahoma, Tennessee, Kentucky, Arkansas.

Publications. Missouri Real Estate Commission Rules and Regulations.

Experience requirements for a broker's license. One year as a salesperson or 40 hours study in real estate.

MONTANA Board of Real Estate
42½ North Main, LaLonde Building
Helena, Montana 59601

Education requirements. Two years of high school or the equivalent education.

Application requirements. Photograph; credit report; $10,000 bond; and recommendation of the licensed broker by whom the applicant will be employed.

Examination information. ETS exam given in 5 sessions per year. The exam writing time is 4 hours. If applicant fails the exam twice, he or she must wait six months before another retake. Calculators permitted.

Fees. Exam fee $25; re-exam fee $20. Original license $25; renewal license $15 for each year.

Continuing education requirements. None.

Residency requirement. None.

Reciprocity. Idaho, North Dakota.

Publications. Directory of Licensees.

Experience requirements for a broker's license. Two years as a salesperson or equivalent education or experience.

NEBRASKA Real Estate Commission
301 Centennial Mall South
Lincoln, Nebraska 68509

Education requirements. High school graduate or certificate of equivalency; 60 classroom hours in a course of study approved by the Commission.

Application requirements. Photograph; credit report.

Examination information. ETS exam given in 10 sessions per year. The exam writing time is 4½ hours. If applicant fails three times, he or she must wait six months before another retake. Calculators permitted.

Fees. Investigation fee $25. Exam fee $50; first re-exam $5; subsequent re-exams $25. Original license $15; renewal license $15 for each year.

Continuing education requirements. None.

Residency requirement. None.

Reciprocity. Arkansas, Georgia, Iowa, Kansas, Maryland, Missouri, New Jersey, New York, Ohio, Oklahoma, Oregon, South Dakota, North Dakota, Utah.

Publications. Nebraska real estate study manual is available; regular newsletter.

Experience requirements for a broker's license. Two years or the equivalent of two years full time. Or 18 credit hours or 180 classroom hours in courses approved by the Commission.

NEVADA Real Estate Division
Department of Commerce
201 South Fall Street
Carson City, Nevada 89710

Education requirements. 90 hours of classroom instruction in real estate principles and law from an approved school.

Application requirements. 2 photographs; notarized affidavit which is part of the application form; written recommendations of at least three resident citizens, not related to the applicant, but who have known him/her for a period of two years or more; and $20,000 recovery fund coverage for which there is a fee of $40.

Examination information. ETS exam given in 6 sessions per year. The exam writing time is 4 hours. Five retakes are permitted per year. Calculators permitted.

Fees. Exam fee $40; re-exam fee $40. Original license $90; renewal license $90 for each two years. Recovery fund assessment $40 for two years.

Continuing education requirements. 20 clock hours within the two-year period immediately after initial license; and 10 clock hours within each subsequent two-year period before renewal.

Residency requirement. Must be resident at the time of application.

Reciprocity. None.

Publications. Regular newsletter.

Experience requirements for a broker's license. Active experience as a licensed salesperson for at least two of the four years previous to application for a broker's license.

NEW HAMPSHIRE	New Hampshire Real Estate Commission 3 Capitol Street Concord, New Hampshire 03301

Education requirements. None.

Application requirements. Affidavits of three residents of the state, owners of real estate in the state, stating that the applicant is of good repute, trustworthy, and entitled to public confidence.

Examination information. ETS exam given in 4 sessions per year. The exam writing time is 4½ hours. If applicant fails two consecutive times, he/she must wait six months before re-application. Calculators permitted.

Fees. Exam fee $25; re-exam fee $25. Original license $30; renewal license $20 for each two years.

Continuing education requirements. None.

Residency requirement. Residency required, but no time period. Non-resident licenses available.

Reciprocity. None.

Publications. Printed material indicating the scope of the state examination and suggested sources of study; Roster.

Experience required for a broker's license. One year full time as a licensed salesperson (or 2,000 hours part time) in New Hampshire or another state or proof of experience equivalent.

NEW JERSEY — New Jersey Real Estate Commission
201 East State Street
Trenton, New Jersey 08625

Education requirements. 45 classroom hours in an approved real estate study course.

Application requirements. Fingerprints; sponsoring broker; and $10,000 recovery fund coverage for which there is a $5 one-time-only fee.

Examination information. ETS exam given in 12 sessions per year. The exam writing time is 4 to 5 hours. No limit on retakes. Calculators permitted.

Fees. Exam fee $13; re-exam fee $13. Original license $15; renewal license $15 for each year.

Continuing education requirements. None.

Residency requirement. None.

Reciprocity. Connecticut, Delaware, Georgia, Kentucky, Massachusetts, Nebraska, New York, North Carolina, Oklahoma, Pennsylvania, Utah, West Virginia.

Publications. New Jersey real estate study manual is available; regular newsletter; Roster.

Experience requirements for a broker's license. Two years apprenticeship under sponsoring broker immediately preceding application for the broker's license.

NEW MEXICO — New Mexico Real Estate Commission
Suite 608
600 Second Street, N.W.
Albuquerque, New Mexico 87102

Education requirements. 60 classroom hours in real estate courses approved by the Commission.

Application requirements. Photograph; fingerprints; credit report; and recommendations of two reputable citizens who own real estate in the county in which the applicant resides.

Examination information. ETS exam given in 12 sessions per year. The exam writing time is 4½ hours. No limit on retakes. Calculators permitted.

Fees. Exam fee $25; re-exam fee $25. Original license $30; renewal license $30 for each year. Recovery fund fee $10 for one year.

Continuing education requirements. None.

Residency requirement. None.

Reciprocity. Partial with California, Colorado, Idaho, Iowa, Kansas, Missouri, Michigan, New Hampshire, New York, North Carolina, Oklahoma, Pennsylvania, Vermont, Virginia.

Publications. License law handbook and educational program handbook; regular newsletter.

Experience requirements for a broker's license. Active experience as a salesperson twenty-four of the preceding thirty-six months in New Mexico; or 180 classroom hours in real estate instruction; or evidence of a broker's license in another state and 90 hours of instruction; or equivalent experience as determined by the Commission.

NEW YORK

Department of State
Real Estate Licensing Office
270 Broadway
New York, New York 10007

Education requirements. 45 hours of approved courses in real estate subjects.

Application requirements. Photograph.

Examination information. ACT exam given in 52 sessions per year. The exam writing time is 1 hour. Three retakes are permitted per application. Calculators permitted.

Fees. No exam fee; re-exam fee $10. Original license $10; renewal license $10 for each two years.

Continuing education requirements. 45 classroom hours every three years.

Residency requirement. None.

Reciprocity. Arkansas, Connecticut, Delaware, District of Columbia, Massachusetts, Nebraska, New Jersey, Ohio, Oklahoma.

Publications. New York real estate study manual is available; regular newsletter.

Experience requirements for a broker's license. One year as a salesperson or two years equivalent experience.

NORTH CAROLINA

Real Estate Commission
1200 Navaho Drive
Post Office Box 17100
Raleigh, North Carolina
27619

Education requirements. 30 classroom hours in real estate or equivalent experience.

Application requirements. Photograph; fingerprints; endorsements of good character by two persons; application fee $20; name and address of broker with whom the applicant is to be associated; and $20,000 recovery fund coverage for which there may be a charge not to exceed $5.

Examination information. ETS exam given in 12 sessions per year. The exam writing time is 4½ hours. Five retakes are permitted per year. Calculators permitted.

Fees. No exam fee; no re-exam fee, but failure of the first re-exam requires re-application and payment of $20 application fee. Original license $20; renewal license $15 for each year.

Continuing education requirements. None.

Residency requirement. None.

Reciprocity. Partial with Arkansas, Connecticut, Delaware, District of Columbia, Georgia, Kentucky, New Jersey, South Carolina, Tennessee, West Virginia.

Publications. Roster of Licensed Salespersons and Brokers; regular newsletter; North Carolina real estate study manual is available.

Experience requirements for a broker's license. Two years sales experience or the equivalent.

NORTH DAKOTA

Real Estate Commission
410 East Thayer Avenue
Post Office Box 727
Bismarck, North Dakota
58502

Education requirements. None.

Application requirements. Application fee $30; and $15,000 recovery fund coverage for which there is a $20 one-time-only fee.

Examination information. ETS exam given in 11 sessions per year. The exam writing time is 4½ hours. Three retakes are permitted; if the third examination is failed the applicant must wait twelve months and then submit a new application. Calculators permitted.

Fees. Exam fee included in application fee; re-exam fee $5. Original license $30; renewal license $20 for each year.

Continuing education requirements. 30 classroom hours completed within one year after date of initial license.

Residency requirement. None.

Reciprocity. Nebraska, Iowa, South Dakota, Minnesota.

Publications. Regular newsletter.

Experience requirements for a broker's license. Two years experience as a licensed salesperson or the equivalent.

OHIO Department of Commerce
Division of Real Estate
180 East Broad Street, 14th Floor
Columbus, Ohio 43215

Education requirements. High school diploma or its equivalent required of all applicants born in 1950 or later; 30 classroom hours in real estate practice and 30 classroom hours in real estate law at an institution of higher learning.

Application requirements. Photograph; and recommendation of employing broker certifying that the applicant is honest, truthful, of good reputation, and has not been convicted of a felony or crime involving moral turpitude, or been in violation of federal or state civil rights laws.

Examination information. Staff or Commission exam given in 80 sessions per year. The exam writing time is 3 hours. No limit on retakes. Calculators permitted.

Fees. Exam fee $27; re-exam fee $27. Original license $27; renewal license $12 for each year.

Continuing education requirements. 30 classroom hours of instruction in each of two courses—real estate appraisal and real estate finance—to be completed within twenty-four months of the date of the original license; and thereafter 30 classroom hours of instruction within each subsequent three-year period.

Residency requirement. None.

Reciprocity. Kentucky, New York.

Publications. Ohio real estate study manual is available; regular newsletter; information booklets.

Experience requirements for a broker's license. Must have been a licensed real estate salesperson in Ohio for at least two of the five years preceding application for a broker's license, and worked as such at least 30 hours per week, and completed at least thirty real estate transactions.

OKLAHOMA

Oklahoma Real Estate Commission
4040 North Lincoln Boulevard, Suite 100
Oklahoma City, Oklahoma 73105

Education requirements. 45 clock hours or 3 semester credit hours in principles of real estate.

Application requirements. Photograph; and $50,000 recovery fund coverage for which there is a $5 fee each year.

Examination information. Staff or Commission exam given in 300 sessions per year. The exam writing time is 3 hours. No limit on retakes. Calculators permitted.

Fees. Exam fee $20; re-exam fee $20. Original license $10; renewal license $10 for each year.

Continuing education requirements. 21 classroom hours every three years.

Residency requirement. None.

Reciprocity. All states.

Publications. Oklahoma real estate study manual is available; License Law Booklet; regular newsletter.

Experience requirement for a broker's license. One year as a licensed sales associate.

OREGON Real Estate Commission
158 12th Street, N.E.
Salem, Oregon 97310

Education requirements. Satisfactory evidence of competence in legal aspects of real estate, real estate practice, and real estate finance, with instruction totaling 90 classroom hours.

Application requirements. None.

Examination information. ACT exam given in 6 sessions per year. The exam writing time is unspecified. No limit on retakes. Calculators permitted.

Fees. Exam fee $25; re-exam fee $25. Original license $60; renewal license $60 for each two-year period.

Continuing education requirements. 24 classroom hours every two-year license period.

Residency requirement. Must establish residency.

Reciprocity. Washington, Idaho.

Publications. Oregon state real estate study manual is available; regular newsletter.

Experience requirements for a broker's license. Engaged in activity as a licensed salesperson at least three years of the five-year period immediately prior to the date of application for a broker's license; or the equivalent experience; or a Bachelor's degree with a major in real estate and one year of experience; or an Associate's degree in real estate and two years of experience.

PENNSYLVANIA Real Estate Commission
Post Office Box 2649
Room 611, Transportation &
Safety Building
Commonwealth Avenue &
Forster Street
Harrisburg, Pennsylvania
17120

Education requirements. 60 classroom hours or 4 college credit hours in real estate study.

Application requirements. Recommendation by employing broker certifying that the applicant is honest, truthful, and of good repute and recommending that the license be granted.

Examination information. ETS exam given in 12 sessions per year. The exam writing time is 4½ hours. Six retakes permitted per year. Calculators permitted.

Fees. Exam fee $20; re-exam fee $10. Original license $20; renewal license $20 for each two years. Recovery fund fee $10 one time only.

Continuing education requirements. None.

Residency requirement. None.

Reciprocity. Partial with Maryland, Delaware, Virginia, Ohio.

Publications. Real Estate Brokers License Act; Rules and Regulations of the State Real Estate Commission.

Experience requirements for a broker's license. Three years full-time apprenticeship or the equivalent.

RHODE ISLAND	Real Estate Division 100 North Main Street Providence, Rhode Island 02903

Education requirements. None.

Application requirements. A statement under oath from the employing broker that, in his opinion, the applicant is competent and trustworthy and is recommended as a suitable person to be granted a salesman's license; and $20,000 recovery fund coverage for which there is a $15 fee.

Examination information. Staff or Commission exam given in 50 sessions per year. The exam writing time is 2 hours. No limit on retakes. Calculators permitted.

Fees. Exam fee $10; re-exam fee $10. Original license $30; renewal license $30 for each year.

Continuing education requirements. None.

Residency requirement. None.

Reciprocity. Connecticut, Massachusetts.

Publications. Real Estate Licensing Laws and Rules and Regulations.

Experience requirements for a broker's license. One year as a licensed salesperson; or baccalaureate degree with a major in real estate; or 90 classroom hours of study in real estate courses approved by the Commission.

SOUTH CAROLINA

Real Estate Commission
2221 Divine Street—
Suite 530
Columbia, South Carolina
29205

Education requirements. 30 classroom hours in a program approved by the Commission, or satisfactory evidence of experience in real estate transactions, or 3 credit hours in real estate at an accredited college.

Application requirements. Photograph; and credit report.

Examination information. University of South Carolina exam given in 12 sessions per year. The exam writing time is 2½ hours. Three retakes are permitted per year. Calculators permitted.

Fees. Exam fee $25; first re-exam no fee; subsequent re-exams $25. Original license $25; renewal license $15 for each year. Credit report fee $5.

Continuing education requirements. None.

Residency requirement. Must be resident.

Reciprocity. Georgia, North Carolina.

Publications. South Carolina real estate study manual is available; regular newsletter.

Experience requirements for a broker's license. Two years experience as a licensed salesperson or 60 hours study in real estate subjects.

SOUTH DAKOTA Real Estate Commission
Post Office Box 490
Pierre, South Dakota 57501

Education requirements. 30 classroom hours in real estate study.

Application requirements. Photograph; credit report; and $15,000 recovery fund coverage for which the fee is pro-rated.

Examination information. ETS exam given in 4 sessions per year. The exam writing time is 4½ hours. One retake is permitted per year. Calculators permitted.

Fees. Exam fee included in original license application fee; re-exam fee $10. Original license $50; renewal license $20 for each year.

Continuing education requirements. 24 hours of instruction every two years.

Residency requirement. None.

Reciprocity. North Dakota, Minnesota, Iowa, Nebraska.

Publications. Regular newsletter.

Experience requirements for a broker's license. Two years as a licensed salesperson.

TENNESSEE Real Estate Commission
556 Capitol Hill Building
Nashville, Tennessee 37219

Education requirements. Self study or 30 hours course work.

Application requirements. Photograph; $2,500 bond.

Examination information. ETS exam given in 12 sessions per year. The exam writing time is 4½ hours. Number of retakes permitted not specified. Calculators permitted.

Fees. Exam fee included in original license fee; re-exam fee $25. Original license $25; renewal license $10 for each year.

Continuing education requirements. 3 college credit hours in real estate or 30 classroom hours of real estate course work within two years of licensure. (This requirement may also be fulfilled before passing the state license exam.)

Residency requirement. Forty-five days prior to issuance of license.

Reciprocity. Full with Arkansas, Georgia, Kentucky, North Carolina. Partial with Virginia.

Publications. Directory of Licensees; *Tennessee Real Estate, The Official Manual of the Tennessee Real Estate Commission.*

Experience requirements for a broker's license. Licensed as an "affiliate broker" [equivalent of a salesperson's license] for two years; or one year's experience and a baccalaureate degree with a major in real estate.

TEXAS Texas Real Estate Commission
Post Office Box 12188, Capitol Station
Austin, Texas 78711

Education requirements. 315 classroom hours or 21 college semester hours credit in real estate course work. As of January 1, 1983: 540 classroom hours or 36 college semester hours. As of January 1, 1985: Broker license only from this date.

Application requirements. Photograph; and $40,000 recovery fund coverage for which a one-time fee of $10 is charged.

Examination information. Staff or Commission exam given in 482 sessions per year. The exam writing time is 2 hours. No limit on retakes. Calculators permitted.

Fees. Application fee $20. Exam fee $5; re-exam fee $5. Original license $20; renewal license $18 each year.

Continuing education requirements. None.

Residency requirement. Sixty days immediately preceding the filing of the application for licensure.

Reciprocity. Partial with California.

Publications. Texas real estate study manual is available; Real Estate License Act; Rules of the Texas Real Estate Commission.

Experience requirements for a broker's license. Two years as an actively licensed salesperson within three years immediately preceding application; or 60 semester hours or 900 classroom hours of acceptable course work.

UTAH Real Estate Division
330 East Fourth South
Salt Lake City, Utah 84111

Education requirements. High school graduation or certificate of General Education Development (G.E.D.) and 90 classroom or 8 college credit hours of approved study in elementary principles and practices of real estate at an approved school.

Application requirements. $6,000 recovery fund coverage for which there is a $5 charge included in the license fee.

Examination information. ACT exam given in 44 sessions per year. The exam writing time is 4 hours, which includes a supplemental state exam. Eleven retakes are permitted per year. Calculators permitted.

Fees. Exam fee $15; re-exam fee $15. Original license $15; renewal license $12 for each year.

Continuing education requirements. None.

Residency requirement. Must be resident for Utah license. Non-resident licenses available.

Reciprocity. Idaho, Washington, Nebraska, Connecticut, Colorado.

Publications. Utah State License Law; Rules & Regulations; Utah Uniform Land Sales Practices Act; Utah Recovery Fund Act; regular newsletter.

Experience requirements for a broker's license. Three years active full-time experience as a licensed salesperson or the equivalent.

VERMONT Executive Secretary
Vermont Real Estate Commission
7 East State Street
Montpelier, Vermont 05602

Education requirements. High school graduate or an equivalent education satisfactory to the Commission.

Application requirements. Photograph; and written statement by the broker whose employ the applicant is to enter stating that in his opinion the applicant is honest, truthful, and of good reputation and recommending that the license be granted.

Examination information. ETS exam given in 4 sessions per year. The exam writing time is 4½ hours. Three retakes are permitted per year. Calculators are *not* permitted.

Fees. Exam fee $25; re-exam fee $25. Original license $15; renewal license $15 for each year.

Continuing education requirements. None.

Residency requirement. Six months. Non-resident licenses are available.

Reciprocity. None.

Publications. Regular newsletter; Roster; Rules & Statutes.

Experience requirements for a broker's license. One year as a licensed salesperson in Vermont.

VIRGINIA Real Estate Commission
2 South 9th Street
Richmond, Virginia 23219

Education requirements. 3 semester hours (6 quarter hours) or 45 classroom hours in principles of real estate courses approved by the Commission.

Application requirements. Written statement of the broker with whom applicant is to be associated stating that in his or her opinion the applicant is honest, truthful, and of good reputation and recommending that the license be granted to the applicant.

Examination information. ETS exam given in 11 sessions per year. The exam writing time is 4½ hours. Five retakes are permitted per year. Calculators permitted.

Fees. Exam fee $55; re-exam fee $25. Original license $30; renewal license $30 for each two years.

Continuing education requirements. None.

Residency requirement. None.

Reciprocity. Delaware, Maryland, Massachusetts, Tennessee, West Virginia, District of Columbia.

Publications. Regular newsletter.

Experience requirements for a broker's license. Three years as a licensed salesperson.

WASHINGTON Real Estate Division
Post Office Box 247
Olympia, Washington 98504

Education requirements. None.

Application requirements. Fingerprints; credit report.

Examination information. Staff or Commission exam given in 12 sessions per year. The exam writing time is 4 hours. No limit on retakes. Calculators permitted.

Fees. Exam fee $25; re-exam fee $25. Original license $25; renewal license $25 for each year.

Continuing education requirements. 30 clock hours in a real estate study program approved by the Commission prior to the second renewal of license.

Residency requirement. Must be permanent resident.

Reciprocity. Partial with Oregon, Idaho, Utah, Georgia.

Publications. Washington real estate study manual is available; regular newsletter; list of approved real estate study courses; other material.

Experience requirements for a broker's license. None.

WEST VIRGINIA

Real Estate Commission
1033 Quarrier Street, Suite 400
Charleston, West Virginia
25301

Education requirements. High school graduate or equivalent; and 90 classroom hours in real estate course work approved by the Commission.

Application requirements. $2,000 bond; and sworn statement by the broker whose employment the applicant is to enter that, in his opinion, the applicant is honest and trustworthy, and recommending the license be granted to the applicant.

Examination information. Staff or Commission exam given in 11 sessions per year. The exam writing time is 4½ hours. One retake per year is permitted. Calculators are *not* permitted.

Fees. Exam fee $25; re-exam no charge. Original license $25; renewal license $25 for one year.

Continuing education requirements. None.

Residency requirement. None.

Reciprocity. District of Columbia, North Carolina, Tennessee, Kentucky, New Jersey, Virginia, Georgia.

Publications. Directory of Licensees.

Experience requirements for a broker's license. Licensed two years as a salesperson.

WISCONSIN Real Estate Commission
Room 281
1400 East Washington
Madison, Wisconsin 53702

Education requirements. None.

Application requirements. Photograph; applicant's signature must be notarized; and voucher: two persons not related to the applicant but residing in the same county as the applicant must sign in the presence of a Notary Public.

Examination information. ACT exam given in 6 sessions per year. The exam writing time is 4½ hours. No limit on retakes. Calculators permitted.

Fees. Exam and re-exam fees included in license fee. Original license $50; renewal license $25 for each two years.

Continuing education requirements. 30 classroom hours within two years after licensing plus 10 classroom hours every two years thereafter.

Residency requirement. None.

Reciprocity. None.

Publications. Wisconsin real estate study manual is available.

Experience requirements for a broker's license. 60 classroom hours in approved real estate courses. No experience.

WYOMING Director of Real Estate
Supreme Court Building
Cheyenne, Wyoming 82002

Education requirements. None.

Application requirements. Photograph; fingerprints; credit report; $1,000 bond; and recommendation of the licensed broker with whom the applicant will be associated stating that in his opinion the applicant is honest, truthful, and of good reputation and recommending that the license be granted to the applicant.

Examination information. ETS exam given in 6 sessions per year. The exam writing time is 4½ hours. No limit on retakes. Calculators are permitted.

Fees. Exam fee $30; re-exam fee $30. Original license $40; renewal license $15 for each year.

Continuing education requirements. None.

Residency requirement. Must be a resident.

Reciprocity. None.

Publications. Wyoming real estate study manual is available; regular newsletter; State correspondence courses are available; Roster of Licensed Brokers and Salespersons; other publications.

Experience requirements for a broker's license. Two years as a full-time salesperson or a degree in real estate from an accredited university or college.

There they are, fifty states and the District of Columbia. If you are like most people, you probably searched the preceding pages to find the licensing information for the state you are now living in and then skipped to this point to begin reading again. But if you happened to look at your neighboring states or skimmed through the whole country, you were probably surprised by the number of states requiring formal class hours in real estate study in addition to requiring a three- or four-hour examination. Formal education requirements for a real estate license are becoming more stringent throughout the country, and many states are now also requiring additional formal classroom study *after* licensing.

Many colleges nationwide list real estate courses in their catalogues, and some universities, including the University of Alabama, the University of Florida, Georgia State University,

Ohio State University, the University of Texas, and the University of Washington, are now offering doctoral degrees in the field. Master's degrees in real estate are offered in at least sixteen colleges and universities across the country, and the Bachelor's degree with a major in real estate is widely offered. Most common of all, however, is the associate (two-year) degree in real estate which is offered at most community colleges.

But college does not necessarily spell success in real estate. In fact a degree or even college-level courses are not a necessity in the field in most states. Many business schools and locally sponsored adult education programs offer courses approved by their state real estate commissions to fulfill pre-licensing requirements, and a few states still require no formal class time at all.

The National Association of Realtors has compiled a list of universities, colleges, and junior colleges across the country that offer on-campus courses in real estate. You can receive the publication without charge by writing and requesting it from:

The Department of Education
National Association of Realtors
155 East Superior Street
Chicago, IL 60611

Most state real estate commissions requiring formal class time also maintain lists of state approved schools which they will mail to you upon request, and often you can find local schools that offer approved pre-license courses advertised in your daily newspaper and/or listed in the yellow pages of your phone book.

What do you learn in the required courses? I bet you thought I was going to say "not much," but that's not true. Most state exams are difficult, with a 40 to 50 percent failure rate not uncommon across the country. The exams do require careful preparation and study, which the courses provide, but the content of that preparation is often theoretical. Ellen Rand, a real estate writer for *The New York Times,* reported in an article on real estate schools that "professionals are quick to point out there is, at best, a tenuous relationship between the course content and the real world."

"What's the 'real world' and why is the relationship so tenuous?" you ask. Well, pre-license course work generally focuses on real estate law and real estate principles, knowledge that is essential to passing the state exam. Most schools, however, make little or no effort to teach methods of handling the day-to-day demands of the job: how to talk with prospective buyers; how to qualify them; how to take a listing at a fair market price; how to negotiate fairly; or how to arrange a mortgage, for example.

It's a little like graduating from college with a degree in English literature and then applying for a teaching job. You know a fair amount about fiction, poetry, and drama, but you still have a long way to go before you master the art of *teaching* English. And in your career in real estate, after you finish your required license preparation course work, and pass your licensing exam, you still have a long way to go before you master the art of selling and listing in the residential marketplace.

FOUR

First Decisions

BEGINNINGS are always tough. Most of us resist making a first decision—from getting out of bed in the morning to getting ourselves wet in a cold shower, or pool, or ocean. But, having made the decision to start a career as a real estate saleswoman, you are over the first hurdle and must now decide which real estate office you wish to work in. Much of your success will depend on this decision.

Getting a job is not the problem. Desks are always available in the real estate world. Since most sales agents work on a commission basis and have frequent contact with agents working in other offices, the grass somehow often looks greener on the other broker's front lawn. There is, therefore, a high turnover rate due to transfers as well as the high dropout rate, and thus the empty desks. It also costs the broker little or nothing to hire a new agent, and by the same token that agent earns nothing until she generates the business that brings commission money into the firm.

So it's not getting a job, it's getting the *right* job that counts. How many hours you work per week in how structured an environment, how much money you make, and how well you learn the realities of the profession and the skills of listing, selling, and negotiating will depend upon the kind of office in which you begin your career.

"Well, what *is* a good office then?" you ask. "What should I look for?"

That depends on the special mix of your personality and needs with the character and policies of the office. Your key to success, to finding a good office, is knowing your own particular needs and goals and how you learn and work best, and then matching that knowledge of yourself with what you can learn about the office and what *it* has to offer. To make this kind of judgment, however, you must know a little about the character of residential real estate offices across the country. There are several main types.

THE NATIONAL FRANCHISE REALTOR

You've watched their spots on television and heard them on the radio; you've read their ads in magazines and newspapers; and you've seen their signs on lawns everywhere. The franchise movement, which began gathering its real strength in the mid-seventies, is now the hottest thing in the real estate business. Each franchise company is spending millions of dollars on creating an image that the home buyer and/or seller will recognize and trust. It's hard to confuse or misinterpret the gold of *Century 21,* the red, white, and blue of *Realty World,* the artist's palette of *Gallery of Homes,* and the happy springtime house of *Better Homes & Gardens,* to name some of the largest. And these images are selling. Independent brokers are joining up everywhere as the public accepts the big name.

What's it all about? Are Mr. & Mrs. John Q. Buyer really in the hands of *Better Homes & Gardens* (of magazine fame) when they enter a white-painted split-level house that has been converted into an office building in a small Iowa town? Not at all.

In virtually all cases, local real estate offices within each franchise remain independently owned and independently run. The firms therefore still reflect the character and efficiency of their individual owners. What those owners buy in joining a franchise, however, is a sign, an image for the public eye, and most important in *their* minds (and in your evaluations) a training program for their sales personnel.

Most brokers nationwide feel that training is the biggest advantage the franchises have to offer, and most who join insist that all their agents take the franchise training courses. These programs are training-to-sell in its slickest, most polished form. If you choose it, you will participate in classes where manuals, selling scripts, video tapes, questionnaires, give-aways, and rallies are a part of the scene. You will probably have a graduation or two, and you will probably receive formal certificates when you complete each course.

Just to give you an idea of the scope of franchise training, let me focus on a fictionalized, but typical, program of a large national franchise that I'll call *Happy Hearth. Happy Hearth* offers a total of 196 class hours of training courses. The program is broken up into various titled and numbered courses given at different times throughout the year. Its completion often takes two years or more, although most agents do not take all the courses. Let's look at an overall outline.

HAPPY HEARTH REAL ESTATE EDUCATION PROGRAM

NEW SALESPERSON ORIENTATION

Prerequisites: Broker must be a member of *Happy Hearth.* Participant must be a licensed real estate salesman/woman under contract with the member broker.

Time: 7 hours.

COURSE 101 LISTING THE HAPPY HEARTH WAY

Prerequisite: New Salesperson Orientation.

Time: 40 hours.

COURSE 102 SELLING THE HAPPY HEARTH WAY

Prerequisites: Course 101 and attendance at 3 *Happy Hearth* rallies.

Time: 40 hours.

COURSE 201 ADVANCED LISTING: WAYS AND MEANS TO THE TOUGH ONES

Prerequisites: Courses 101 and 102, nine months' experience, attendance at 5 *Happy Hearth* rallies, and six listings to your credit.

Time: 18 hours.

COURSE 202 ADVANCED SELLING: HOW TO GET THOSE DEALS TOGETHER

Prerequisites: Courses 101 and 102, nine months' experience, attendance at 5 *Happy Hearth* rallies, and six sales to your credit.

Time: 18 hours.

COURSE 300 MANAGEMENT TECHNIQUES

Prerequisites: Courses 101, 102, 201, and 202, one year's experience in residential sales, and recommendation of the employing broker.

Time: 30 hours.

COURSE 401 COMMERCIAL SALES, LISTING AND BROKERAGE

Prerequisites: Courses 101, 102, 201, 202, one year's experience in residential sales, and recommendation of the employing broker.

Time: 25 hours.

COURSE 402 ADVANCED COMMERCIAL BROKERAGE

Prerequisite: Course 401 and a broker's or associate broker's license.

Time: 18 hours.

Impressive outline, isn't it? But you're probably wondering, "What can take up forty hours that I can't learn on the job?" Let's look a little closer at *Course 101: Listing the Happy Hearth Way.* Here's another outline.

LISTING THE HAPPY HEARTH WAY

10 Seminars Each 4 Hours

1. OBJECTIVES—THINKING RIGHT!

   Setting goals; managing time; your positive attitude. Believe!

2. THE LISTING FARM

   Where do I find the gold in them thar hills?

3. How to Do It
   Leads, knowing yourself, showing and selling your company.

4. Canvassing
   Getting prepared, using your resources, practicing telephone conversations, door-to-door techniques, precautions.

5. Sellers Advertising for a Broker
   Finding those For-Sale-by-Owner people, telephone contact, personal contact, follow-ups, giving advice.

6. The MLS Records and Where They Lead
   Expired listings, expired withdrawals, sales three years past. How to make the approach and sell yourself and your company.

7. Changing an Unsatisfied Buyer Into a Seller
   Money talk, mortgages, closing and occupancy as a negotiating tool, how to protect your time investment.

8. Happy Hearth and Why We're The Best
   Listing scripts, the presentation book, rehearsals, and evaluations.

9. Answers to Every Objection
   Discussion, role-playing, and aids for getting those signatures.

10. Final Exam
    Luncheon, prizes, graduation.

When you finish your ten weeks in Course 101, you can't help but have a feeling for listing the *Happy Hearth* way. Each of the courses in the *Happy Hearth* education program is as carefully planned and thorough as this one. It is a professional program that few small independent brokers could put together on their own, even if they had the time.

I have personally attended classes under a franchise program and I must admit I was impressed with the training. Its weakness, however (and everything in real estate has a weakness or two), is that it is highly patterned and programmed. You learn what to do in the theoretical normal situation, and you learn it well, but what happens when things *aren't* normal? Where do you learn to handle problems, for example, that don't appear in the Objections List? *Not normal* is so common in real estate as to be almost the normal, and a well-trained agent must learn to think independently as well as memorize lists and procedures.

Let's say you have a sticky problem. If the franchise-member broker for whom you work is conscientious, he/she will be available and willing to help you, to share his/her experience with you, in order to resolve the situation. If this happens, the broker will very much earn the office share of the commission you bring in. If, however, you work in an office where training is completely turned over to the franchised program and the broker or office manager is unavailable as a teacher and guide, you may find the going rather difficult. Textbooks and class work rarely answer specific and/or unusual questions.

And how about the work? In general, franchised offices are rather structured. You may not punch a time clock, but certain hours per week will be expected of you. There are also numerous staff meetings and procedural policies, and numerous titles and positions. Even in the smallest franchise office, someone other than the member broker must be designated "office manager" and someone must be designated "relocation specialist." In larger franchised firms—those that have several offices under one broker membership—your contact with the owning broker is often minimal, and the character of the individual office becomes more dependent upon the personality of the office manager. There is also a good amount of extra paperwork required by the franchises such as referral forms, time sheets, opinion gathering, and follow-up procedures. In general, then, work in a franchised office is rather impersonal, although in actual practice, of course, you may find individual offices that are very supportive and warm.

THE MULTI-OFFICE INDEPENDENT REALTOR

There's a growing feeling among brokers that the way to survive without joining a franchise is to open a dozen or more offices of their own. Bigness is definitely "in."

If you join a large independent firm (three offices or more and expanding), you will seldom see the broker (or brokers) whose name appears on the sign under which you work. Most likely, he, she, or they will have long since lost contact with the day-to-day mechanisms of selling houses in order to concentrate upon administering the growing empire. The office in which you work will be run by an office manager, who in turn will probably be responsible to other managers and directors and be guided by a detailed company policy manual. The large multi-office firm is very much the equivalent in the real estate world of working for the large national corporation.

Most of these large firms offer company-written and company-run training programs which cover much of the same ground as the franchise programs which I described, but usually with a little less gingerbread and gilt. Generally these are good programs and they offer you the added advantage of training alongside the people with whom you will be working. You will also have the advantage of beginning in a program closely geared to the needs and character of your local area.

Much of your success or failure and happiness or dissatisfaction while working for a multi-office organization will depend upon the office manager in your particular office. Like the broker in the one-office firm who joins a franchise, the office manager in the multi-office firm will set the tone of the office in which he/she works. His or her personality and dedication can, and often will, make the difference for you between getting the help you need to learn the business and thrashing about trying to keep your head above water.

One of the problems, or weaknesses, in multi-office organizations is that office managers leave, or are transferred, or start their own businesses much more frequently than brokers who are running their own small businesses. For you as a working saleswoman, a manager's leaving might mean that you will have to adjust to a change of office style under a new manager, or it might mean that you too will leave the firm to follow an office manager with whom you have enjoyed working.

There is usually even more structure in the multi-office firm than in the one-office franchise member. You will have specific hours, days off, vacation times, and always company policy. On the other hand, the big organization offers you the security of a designated and defined niche, of knowing where you are and what you are supposed to be doing. It can also offer advantages in group life and health insurance.

THE SMALL INDEPENDENT REALTOR

I worked for a short time in a small office where I was the only residential sales agent. The broker made his living in that office and often showed houses and took listings himself. His wife was a licensed salesperson also, but she never showed property. She came to the office to answer the phone and keep the files up to date.

There was no formal training program in this small office, but working there was an excellent learning experience. The broker knew every customer I was working with by name, exactly where I was in every deal, and every listing possibility that I had. He openly shared his knowledge and experience with me and often made suggestions for handling every difficult (and sometimes not-so-difficult) situation. I was doing well; yet, finally, I left.

Why? I felt I was being suffocated, or to use another image, I felt the reins were being held too tightly. I felt constantly watched, and became more and more fearful of making mistakes. And I resented that fear. Everyone in real estate makes mistakes or misjudgments—it's part of the game—and everyone must learn to handle the realization that "This one might have gone better."

My next stop on the real estate working circuit was another small independently owned office. This time I was one of six salespeople who kept the office open on a rotating floor-time schedule. Usually, there was only one person in that office at a time—the one assigned to floor time. It was a lonely job. Our broker dropped in once or twice a day between golf, tennis, or handball matches, and sometimes his wife even popped in to see how things were going. Needless to say there was plenty of opportunity to make mistakes and a rather free rein.

These two offices were the opposite poles among small independent real estate firms, but each type is found just as frequently as the more ideal broker who stands midway between them. That ideal broker is the one who is there to instruct and support, but who allows his/her people the freedom to make some decisions (and of course some mistakes) on their own.

Structured training programs are very rare in small one- or two-office firms. Some brokers do encourage their sales agents to read from a more or less well-chosen office library or to enroll in out-of-office continuing education programs. And some will even split the cost of these programs with their sales agents.

The finest of the continuing education programs is sponsored by the Realtor Institute of the National Association of Realtors. Its GRI (Graduate Realtor Institute) designation is respected everywhere as an emblem of superior training and knowledge. The course work focuses on real estate law, housing problems, appraisal, principal and agent relationship, and matters of professional knowledge and service, with minimal attention to selling techniques. The program was designed for national homogeneity, but the Realtor Institute allows each local Realtor Board the option of expanding, contracting, or slightly varying it within given limits to fit the needs of their local area. In general the program follows a three-course outline, totaling ninety hours of classroom instruction.

In addition to the GRI progam, "seminars" (sometimes very high-priced) are offered throughout the country and throughout the year by "expert" sales agents or "expert" listers. These people are usually expert lecturers who have developed teaching programs. Some are good and worth their fee; others are not.

Just as the small independent firm usually demands little or no time commitment to formal training sessions, it also demands minimal formal commitment to office hours. Rarely are hours designated for sales meetings, or listings reviews, or caravans, or canvassing. Rarely are days off named. The salesperson is often free to arrange her own time and work schedule.

Usually if you choose to work in a small independent Realtor office, you will have the greatest freedom and time flexibility. It is the type of office most conducive to part-time work or to arranging full-time hours to suit the needs of a special life-style. It is sometimes the least supportive, however. You may truly be an independent contractor, more or less on your own, and the business you do will come primarily as a result of your own resources and efforts.

REALTORS

Did you notice that the last three headings all contained the word "Realtor"? Many people have come to think of any licensed person who sells real estate as a realtor. But in fact the assumption is untrue. The word Realtor is a registered trademark of the National Association of Realtors. The NAR is a trade group of member brokers who subscribe to a professional code of ethics. Technically only member *brokers* can call themselves Realtors; sales agents in the employ of those brokers are called "Associate Realtors," although in common usage, they are often called Realtors too.

Being a Realtor or working for one almost invariably means membership in and access to a Multiple Listing Service. Through the network of Realtor Boards across the country, Multiple Listing has become so common a practice in residential real estate that most buyers and sellers have come to take it for granted. In reality the marketplace is not so tranquil, however, as there are movements afoot to establish alternatives to MLS and legal battles being fought over who may join MLS and who may use its information.

FEE BROKERS

Fee brokers have been around in the real estate business for more than twenty years, but not until recently have they received serious attention. The spotlight has focused upon them now because they are growing in number and popularity and perhaps because the general public is looking for money-saving alternatives during difficult financial times.

A fee broker does just what the name implies: he/she charges a fee for his service rather than a commission based upon a percentage of the selling price of the property. The fees and the services provided vary tremendously across the country. *Home Sellers Centers,* which is a national franchise of fee brokers, charged, during 1980, a flat fee of $1,000 to handle a house. At the same time, *Equity Savers,* an independent firm in San Antonio, Texas, was charging a flat fee of $350 paid on signing the listing contract, or a sliding fee (from $500 to $900 depending on the sale price of the house) at closing.

At *Equity Savers* and most other fee brokers, sales agents do *not* show houses. The sellers do their own showing. Agents take listings, advertise, and help with the negotiating and contracts.

Most fee brokers have some individualized training programs for new salespeople since their marketing policies and procedures are rather different from the traditional approach to home sales. Their emphasis is on volume and quick turnover, and because their customers must go out and find the properties on their own, their appeal is primarily to local buyers. It is a fast-paced, highly competitive business with income dependent on quantity of business much more than quality of service.

I do not recommend a fee brokerage house as a place to start in the real estate business because much of the training you get there will have to be unlearned if you decide later to work with a traditional Realtor and member of a Multiple Listing Service. (And the business failure rate among fee brokers is extremely high.)

SPECIALISTS

Across the country, but especially near vacation areas and in large cities, there are many licensed brokers who are not Realtors, or members of the local Multiple Listing Service, or discount fee brokers, or, in fact competitive in any way in the race for residential listings. Their sales agents rarely drive farther while on the job than the distance between their homes and the office, and their hours are absolutely regular. "Impossible in this business," you say. Yet in truth these brokers run successful residential offices, *specialized offices.*

By specialized offices I mean those brokers who are the *exclusive* agents for the sale of, let's say, a massive residential development in Florida, or a huge condo complex in Chicago, or a recreation paradise in the Poconos, or ranchettes in Arizona. I'm sure you get the idea. The sales agents who work in their firms never shop for product (listings) to sell, because product is built into the very existence of the firm. In fact, many of the "brokerage" firms are but wholly owned subsidiaries of the development corporation.

Some of the sales agents for specialized brokers work on site, both showing and selling the property that the firm handles. Others work out of state, with prospects gathered together at special parties or presentations.

As a place to learn the real estate business, the specialized brokerage house leaves much to be desired since its training is necessarily narrow. But if you are looking for part-time employment with regular hours and minimal competition, it *can* offer you the opportunity for extra income.

LEASING AGENTS

In large cities some brokers specialize exclusively in rental property, that is *everything* from two-room flats, to lofts, to penthouses, to sublets of expensive condominiums, to whole apartment complexes which they also manage, to floor space and sometimes whole buildings for commercial use. The field is similar in most ways to residential sales except that you deal in leases rather than contracts of sale and that your commissions are usually smaller but more frequent. If you live in one of this country's largest cities, you may find that work with a leasing broker is both excellent training and financially rewarding.

MAKING YOUR CHOICES

Now that we've glimpsed the workings of the various types of real estate offices, you're probably looking again at your own goals and needs and personality traits and thinking, "Well, I need a little more time to *think* about this." You'd probably like to spend a few days working in each office to try it out, right?

I can't blame you, but unfortunately in the majority of states in this country, the decision "Whom do I work for?" has to be made even before you file your application for a salesperson's license since an employing broker must sponsor and recommend each applicant. And even in those states which do not require a sponsoring broker, the decision must be made soon after licensing, for no licensed *salesperson* can conduct business in real estate in any state except in the employment and under the supervision of a licensed *broker.* Everywhere there are fees for transferring a salesperson's license from one broker to another, and everywhere there are laws stating that a salesperson may work in the employment of only *one* licensed broker (or firm) at any given time.

So you must choose based on the information you can gather. You now know the major types of offices in residential real estate; your next step is to choose among them and then to find the individual office in which you would like to start your career.

After you have narrowed down your decision of type, the tools for scouting individual offices are very simple: the yellow pages of your phone book; the real estate section of your newspaper; and your friends and acquaintances.

The yellow pages are a good starting point because the ads there are not cluttered with the details of houses for sale. Most display ads will include the franchise association, if any, the relocation services to which the broker belongs, the addresses and phone numbers of all branch offices, and usually the name of the broker who owns and/or operates the firm. Thumbing through the pages, you can make a list of all the firms which seem to fall into the category or type that you have chosen.

Now begin eliminating from the list those offices not acceptable to you. The first criterion for elimination should be location. I can't stress strongly enough that you should choose to work at a firm close to your home. In a job that requires a considerable amount of driving anyway, you certainly don't want to add unnecessary distance between home and office to your gas bill. Important as fuel economy is, however, it is not the primary reason for choosing a broker close to home.

Here's the big reason. When you choose the agency for which you will work, you also choose your real estate marketplace. Residential real estate is a *local* business. People list their houses with offices that are nearby and they shop for houses with sales agents who know a local area. You will be most successful and find breaking into your career easiest if you work in an office located in an area you know intimately. Your listing sources will be expanded to include friends, business associates of yourself and your family, and neighbors, and your selling tools will include all the warmth and color that you have discovered in your years of living in the area.

After you narrow your list of potential work places down to those located within a reasonable distance of your home, use the real estate pages of your newspaper to gather a little more information about each firm. Follow the ads (it's a good idea to clip those that interest you) and evaluate the frequency of the advertising, the location of the listings, the type of houses advertised, and the tone of the advertising (high pressure, slick, sophisticated, warm, honest, etc.). You will begin to get glimpses of where certain agencies are strong and where they are weak, and a feel for the character of the various firms. Collect your clippings and write out informal profiles of what *you* think of each firm. This kind of careful study and evaluation can only help you when you finally walk through their doors for your first interview.

And now your friends. If you are lucky enough to know someone who works in a real estate office, take her/him out to lunch. Then ask questions, lots of them. This luncheon will be a practice run for your interviews and a great time to gather information. Some questions to consider: What kind of floor-time schedule is used? How often must an agent work weekends? What is the training program like? How much supervision and assistance is there? How many meetings? What kind of commission splits? Is there an incentive program? What procedure is used for covering when you can't be in a particular place at a particular time? What kind of clerical support? How many other sales agents in the office? *Do you like working there? Why?*

If you know no one who works in a real estate office, ask friends or acquaintances who have recently bought or sold houses what they thought of the various agencies and agents they worked with. If they give you names of agents they particularly liked, don't hesitate to call and ask to meet the agent and talk about your career plans. Some may tell you they're just too busy, but others will be happy to help.

In your quest for the right real estate broker, don't be overly impressed with advertisements for new agents in the Help Wanted section of your local newspaper. Some firms advertise for new agents on a more or less regular basis, but the absence of advertisement does *not* necessarily mean that all the other firms are closed to new applicants. In real estate the best way to find out if there's a desk available is to apply. When you have chosen the best four or five firms to suit your needs, goals, and personality, phone each and make an appointment for an interview.

Perhaps you are thinking that I've spent a lot of time on choosing an office. "Why not just pick one and get started? You can always change later," you say. Well, you could, and in fact many people do just that, but as I mentioned earlier, *40 percent* drop out in their first year. The first year in the real estate business is difficult no matter where you work, but being choosy about *where* can make a tremendous difference in *how* difficult.

FIVE

Getting Started

I ONCE read a survey which asked people what they feared most. The most common answer was not death, or pain, or loneliness, or war. It was *speaking before a group*! There seems to be something about standing up there, being looked at, and listened to, and evaluated that gets the adrenalin flowing and the pulse pounding. It's the classic fight or flight pattern.

For many people a job interview is very much like standing up to speak before a group. Applicants feel the spotlight is turned on high and focused and they must perform and be judged. And they are fearful. And it shows.

One applicant speaks with a shaky, breathless voice and a hundred uhms and ahs. Another twists her rings around and around on her finger as she answers each question. Yet another sits bolt upright on the edge of the chair without so much as twitching a muscle, whereas the person who preceded her couldn't find a comfortable way to keep her feet. And then there is the woman who repeats and clarifies every answer to every question with "yes, but," "and also," "you understand," "except when," "most of the time unless of course," . . . etc., etc.

Nervousness manifests itself in a multitude of symptoms, all of which are painfully obvious and all of which tend to detract from the applicant's hoped-for good impression. First impressions are important in every job interview, but they are crucial in a sales-related job. Sales agents must not appear nervous when they meet new people.

All right, *you* want a job in real estate sales and you don't want nervousness to hurt your chances of getting the job you want. How do you keep your body from giving you away? The answer is in your head. To stop acting nervously, *stop thinking anxiously.*

I know, I know. You're sitting there saying to yourself, "That's easy for her to say. She only has to write it down. She doesn't have to sit there on the wrong side of a desk while someone fires questions at her!"

That's true, right at this moment. But I have sat on that wrong side of the desk many times and I've discovered during those sittings that the secret of a successful interview is a matter of attitude, your attitude. People respond physically to what they are thinking. To be successful in eliminating your nervousness, therefore, think of the interview as a positive experience, an experience over which you have every bit as much control as your prospective employer. Here's how:

Remember first that the word "interview" when divided into syllables breaks down to mean "to see between." *Between* is the important word here, the word that will help determine your attitude. Remember it and go to every *inter*-view knowing that the seeing and the looking at is mutual, a view shared *between* the participants. Yes, you are being evaluated, but you are also evaluating your potential employer, the company, and the job. Don't be afraid to ask yourself, "What's in this for me?" No one else can or will ask that question as well as you. And while you are asking it, your nervousness will evaporate. *You* will be in control.

Another important step in achieving an attitude of security and control during an interview is role-playing. Before your interview, try to think about the job and the interview from the employer's side of the desk. What is the broker likely to be looking for, judging? Then try out the standards and categories and questions that you think of as a broker against your evaluation and knowledge of yourself. To help you get started, I've listed some of the most common checkpoints with some suggestions on how to handle and think about them.

YOUR APPEARANCE

Do you worry about your weight? Your height? The color of your hair, the texture of your skin, the size of your nose? Everyone does—and no one should. No one, that is, except those few women whose livelihood depends upon their physical appearance: the fashion models, ballet dancers, and cover girls among us. For the rest of us, personal appearance is a factor in the way we are evaluated, but the evaluation has little to do with high school prom queen standards of beauty.

The personal appearance evaluation that counts in an interview is the overall feeling that the prospective employer gets upon first seeing you. It doesn't matter if you're fat or thin, short or tall, fair or dark. It does matter that when you walk through the office door, you give an immediate impression of professionalism and competence, and something else, something not so easy to sum up in a word or phrase. Strange as this may sound, that something else in your appearance is the thing that makes your prospective employer feel comfortable, comfortable with the thought of seeing you about the office every working day, comfortable with the thought of you as a member of his/her staff.

Now professionalism, or competence, or being comfortable with a person does not depend upon whether or not she wears a size 7 dress, or just paid $30 to have her hair styled, or uses a $19-an-ounce moisturizer on her face each night. No, your appearance will generate acceptance and approval only if it is a genuine mirror and demonstration of your own self-confidence.

In other words, to make that person on the other side of the desk feel comfortable with you, you must feel comfortable with yourself. You must love and approve of yourself, and when you do, you'll find success not only in your interviews but also with the customers or clients with whom you work.

"Love yourself" is, of course, good advice always, everywhere, and can be found as the dominant theme of just about every self-help popular psychology book on the market today.

But how about some props on the way to that goal? What concrete steps can a woman take to feel better about herself and improve that initial response to her appearance as she walks through the door to her job interview? Let's begin with your clothes.

For that interview day, choose an outfit that you feel proud of and that fits well. Remember your attire should be the feminine counterpart of a man's business suit. A lime-green skirt or an op-art print dress will not make anyone's eyes comfortable. Keep your color and style choices moderate and modest. The latest high-fashion import from Paris, or a pair of sleek designer stretch jeans, or a plunging neckline lace-edged blouse, or sky-high strap sandals will all score minus points for you in a professional office, though each might be appropriate and attractive somewhere else. Try for a look that is neat, tailored, well coordinated, and most of all easy. Easy to be with, easy to look at, easy to wear.

Your jewelry should complement you and your outfit, and never be overwhelming. Your shoes and bag should be color coordinated and—I hate the word, but here it is most appropriate—*sensible.* Remember a real estate agent walks miles a day, in and out of houses, up and down stairs, and sore feet can shorten both one's patience and perseverance.

If you choose to wear perfume, it should be the faintest hint of something pleasant in the air. There is nothing more devastating to a prospective employer's evaluation than being overwhelmed (choked?) with "sexy" musk and flowers as an applicant approaches.

Your hair should be clean above all and styled in a way that feels natural for you. Avoid the just-out-of-the-beauty-parlor look. Likewise with makeup. Wear what you feel comfortable with, but stop short of three-quarter-inch eye lashes and "velvet violet" eye shadow.

And smile! A firm handshake, a warm smile, and a pleasant conversational voice do more to leave the impression of an attractive and competent person than all the cosmetics and clothing money can buy.

YOUR SKILLS

A membership profile published by the National Association of Realtors in 1978 is full of surprising facts and statistics about the people in real estate sales. Would you guess, for example, that nine out of every ten sales associates had tried another career before entering real estate? And many had tried several. Here is an approximate breakdown by percentage.

Secretarial/Bookkeeping	16.0
Management	10.3
Sales	8.6
Teaching	8.6
Retailing	5.8
Government	4.5
Armed Forces	4.4
Insurance	3.7
Banking/Finance	3.2
Building	2.2
Communications	1.9
Accounting	1.7
Farming	1.2
Engineering	1.1
Other	26.8

I've included the list here because I want to emphasize that your life experience skills are an important part of your qualification for a real estate sales position. The role of a real estate agent demands such a wide variety of skills that almost any career experience adds strength to some aspect of your qualifications. And do not discount volunteer or club work. A conscientious volunteer or club officer who has worked well with associates and the general public stands tall in the eyes of an employing broker.

One of the largest working groups from which new real estate agents are drawn is usually disregarded as a profession (it doesn't even appear on the National Association of Realtors list). And, strangely enough, even its members tend to forget or disregard the skills it demands. The profession, of course, is homemaker. Do not hesitate to list "homemaker" among your credentials and include the fact that you have raised or are raising one, two, three, or more children. Include their present ages and the fact that you have been a Cub Scout or Brownie leader, or soccer coach, or 4-H advisor. These activities demand skill, dedication, perseverance, and community involvement—all pluses in a job interview.

One word of caution, however: if your children are young (pre-school or early elementary grades), be prepared to explain the arrangements you have made for child care. Yes, the question is unfair, but it *will* be asked, either aloud or silently in the mind of your prospective employer, and you will fare better if you can erase any doubts by anticipating it.

Before your first interview, type a summary of your previous employment and make several Xerox-type copies of it. Take one with you to each interview. You can then attach it to your application form. This will cut down writing time in filling out the form *and* it will allow you to describe each job in terms of the specific skills and responsibilities involved. You might also take along copies of a letter or two of recommendation if you have them.

Do not, however, rely solely upon this written material. You must be ready, willing, and able to talk about your previous occupation(s). What did you find most satisfying in the job(s)? What did you like least? What skills did you learn and how did you grow as a person in each? Why did you leave the position(s)? Why do you think you can succeed in real estate sales?

These are questions you will most likely be asked, and you will make a better impression at your interview if you have the answers ready. A good way to get ready is to engage the help of a friend. Ask that friend to play the role of your potential employer, give him/her a list of possible questions and free rein to think of and add others, and then conduct a mock interview. You'll be even better prepared if you do this with two or three friends at different times and in different places, for you'll begin to get a sense of the dynamics involved in responding to individual personalities and questioning methods.

YOUR GOALS

The brokers' favorite question, "Why do you think you can succeed in real estate sales?" really asks for more than an evaluation of your skills. Implicit in the question are several other questions. What do you consider success? How much time are you willing to devote to its pursuit? What is it about the career that attracts you? All of these are questions you should work through before you plunge into the job, or even before you plunge into applying for the job. Your answers will affect not only the impression you make during your interview but also the way you feel about your work for the first year or so.

Does success mean money to you? If so, and if you hope to get rich quick as a real estate agent, you had better stop now. There is a living to be made and a good one in the field, but it is the extremely rare agent who sports about in a Mercedes.

During 1981 the National Association of Realtors will be compiling information from a new survey of real estate agents, but for the time being the latest available figures on salaries appear in their *Membership Profile 1978*, and these statistics are from the 1977 fiscal year. In that year, the middle 50 percent of sales agents made between $9,000 and $21,000. Add four years of inflation to those figures and you'll come up with something in the mid-teens to high twenties. Not bad, but certainly *not* riches! On the other hand, you should remember that *usually* in a commission-based profession, those who work harder get paid more.

If, on the other hand, you see success as fame or recognition, a real estate career may or may not be for you. You may make the million dollar club, you could be elected Realtor of the Year, and you may even get your picture in the local newspapers occasionally, but generally your recognition in this business comes in small doses.

Success in real estate equals deals made. Deals made means income from commissions earned for services performed for buyers and sellers. Success therefore is both in your pocketbook and in the sincere expressions of gratitude for a job well done. But there are plenty of deals that fall apart, plenty of times when you just can't get the house that a couple wants at a price they can afford.

Time is the counterpoint of money in considering your real estate goals. Usually the more time you devote to the job the higher your income. But how important is the job to you? What part do you want it to play in your life? Are you willing to devote evenings and weekends to running down leads or putting together deals?

According to the National Association of Realtors' statistics, the median hours worked per week among real estate sales agents is, believe it or not, 40. Just like everyone else. But in this case the median is somewhat deceptive, for the range of hours spent varies widely. More than one third of the sales associates surveyed worked at least 50 hours a week and 16.8 percent worked 60 hours or more a week. On the other end of the curve, one quarter worked less than 30 hours per week, and 13.1 percent worked less than 20 hours.

And remember, none of these figures represents a nine-to-five day. There is great flexibility and much free time in real estate; there are also long days and skipped lunches.

Where do you want to fit in? You must consider the question. Consider it while you are cleaning your house, or preparing a walnut torte for a special dinner party, or enjoying a novel in the hammock on a warm summer Sunday. A commitment to a successful career in real estate means giving up some of life's other activities. Try to evaluate the time commitment you are willing to make *before* you approach your first interview. Your prospective employer will want to talk about it with you and it is important that you have some standards of your own when he or she presents the office floor-time and working-hours schedule.

THE VIEW FROM YOUR SIDE OF THE DESK

We've been focusing upon how *you* will look to the broker during your interview, but as it is an *inter*view, it's now time to discuss how the broker will look to you. You are acquiring a first impression of him/her as a person and evaluating his or her appearance just as much as you are being evaluated. And you too should feel comfortable with the person for whom you choose to work. Not only will you see your broker or office manager often each working day, but you will also take direction and seek help from him/her.

Don't be shy about asking some questions of your interviewer. How long has he/she been in the business? Did he or does he now list, show, and sell houses? Is the business primarily residential sales or is the broker also involved in commercial sales and leases? And ask about the office characteristics discussed in Chapter 4. How large is the staff? Is there a training program? Does the broker plan a franchise involvement in the future? Or does he plan to open more offices independently? Does he tend to specialize in a particular area or type of property?

Try to get a feeling both for the personality of your interviewer and for the office itself. And don't be afraid to trust your instincts. If you come away from an interview feeling that everything about the office sounded fine, but somehow you just weren't able to communicate, weren't comfortable, with the broker, look elsewhere before you decide. And on the other hand, if you come away thinking the office has some shortcomings, but the broker was a dynamic, enthusiastic individual who put you at ease and gave you confidence, don't cross the firm from your list of possibilities.

Since you are going into your interview already knowing the general type of firm you have chosen, you can and should spend some time asking questions about the particulars of work in that specific office. Essentially, it all breaks down to questions of time and money.

TIME

One of your first questions should concern how your prospective broker manages floor time because floor time in real estate is a stepping stone to commission checks. As I mentioned in Chapter 1, floor time in most offices means that you must be *in* the office and that all prospective business generated during that specified period is yours. The question is: What is the specified period? Some brokers assign each agent a full day. Others use four-hour shifts. Some brokers rotate the phone calls among those agents who happen to be in the office at any given time, and in some very small agencies the broker simply doles out the leads even if the sales agent is *not* in the office.

The plan that you prefer will probably depend upon your life-style. If you have small children, you may find it easier to get a sitter for one full day a week, than, say, two four-hour stretches on different days. If you are an older person, or if you are involved in many community activities, you may prefer to work in an office that assigns floor time in two- or three-hour shifts several days a week. If you have a great deal of open time and can be in the office conveniently, you might even prefer taking your turn at answering the phone as a plan.

Try to make an evaluation of your time needs before your interview so that you have a goal in mind and can then discuss it with the prospective broker. Some brokers, even in this high pressure age, are willing to make accommodations for agents with time problems, especially if those problems and their potential solutions are presented and discussed in advance of employment.

Once you determine the floor-time plan, ask how soon you will be allowed to participate. Most of the large multi-office companies and many of the franchise offices do not allow new agents floor time until a fair amount of training has been completed. I even heard of one firm that did not allow an agent floor time until she had brought *five* new listings into the office. Another firm required four weeks of listening in on the phone conversations of experienced agents before allowing the new agent to answer a call.

Generally, the requirements are much less stringent in small one-office independents and in rural offices. In fact there you might even get assigned floor time on your first day on the job, and that, believe me, can be an unnerving experience.

Weekend floor time is usually scheduled differently from

the work-week pattern and it is a good idea to ask about it. Few agents want to spend weekends sitting in the office; it's either a time for showing and selling houses or for getting away to enjoy a little leisure. And believe it or not, phone calls and walk-ins are usually few. So try for an office where weekend duty is required only once or twice a month.

Also ask about days off. Most competent brokers realize that everyone needs time away from the job. Each sales agent should have one weekday off to compensate for the weekend time she invariably puts in. On that day, there should be someone else assigned to handle her calls and attend to all the time-sensitive emergencies that invariably come up.

MONEY

Many people think real estate sales agents make a lot of money. They think so because they see the 6 percent commission on a $100,000 house as $6,000, and that's a lot of money, especially if a particular agent just sold you a house in only two days. Those buyers often get to thinking, "Wow! That gal is good! She probably sells six or seven houses a month! Man, at that rate she must make . . ."

But whoa! Let's assume you sold that $100,000 house with a 6 percent commission. What really happens to that $6,000? If the broker for whom you work is a Realtor and a member of a Multiple Listing Service, there is a very good chance that the house you sold was listed by another agency. This means the commission is split between the listing broker and the selling broker at a rate predetermined and agreed upon. The split may be fifty-fifty, or sixty-forty (in favor of the selling broker), or even seventy-thirty.

Let's say it's fifty-fifty. This means $3,000 of that commission remains with the selling agency (yours). Now if that agency is a franchise member, a certain agreed-upon percentage or amount of that income goes immediately to the franchise headquarters, let's say 3 percent. This means $2,910 remains in your office. Whether or not your agency is a franchise member, the broker may charge an office maintenance fee, say 1½ percent ($43.65). This leaves $2,866.35. This cash is then divided between the broker and the sales agent according to their prior agreement. The most common division is fifty-fifty, leaving the sales agent with $1,433.18, a far cry from the up-front figure of $6,000.

This is a typical story. There are many, many variations on it, however. Often there are multiple listing service fees to be deducted, and sometimes other expenses are incurred in the course of the transaction which the broker insists be split between the office and the sales agent. Even the fifty-fifty left-over commission split between broker and sales agent has many variations. Some brokers offer sixty-forty (60 percent to the sales agent after deductions) right from the start. Other brokers have incentive programs such as a fifty-fifty split for the first $20,000 of gross commission money brought into the office per year, sixty-forty for the next $20,000, and seventy-thirty for everything over $40,000 gross. Still other firms keep the commission split constant, but use a bonus system. And a very few brokers allow sales agents to keep the whole of their earned commissions in return for paying the broker a stipulated monthly fee for desk space, phone use, advertising, and miscellaneous expenses.

It is obviously important that you discuss the commission-split program in an office before you begin work. And then, get it in writing. Written contracts of employment between broker and sales agent were rare when I began work as an agent twelve years ago; today they are prevalent across the country. And they should be. A statement in writing can save untold agony over a commission dispute or the status of active listings when a sales agent leaves a firm.

The Realtor Associations of most states have printed contracts of employment available into which specific conditions can be typed and agreements on commission splits stated. It is especially important that these contracts include statements defining the status and disposition of incomplete transactions and transactions pending closing in the event that a sales agent leaves a firm. A good example of such a clause might be:

> Incomplete transactions are defined as those in which there has been no signed agreement, and therefore there is no commission

> due the employed salesperson. A property under contract to purchase is considered a completed transaction and subject to payment of commission after closing. A listing is considered a completed transaction if it is sold at any time during the entire term of the listing agreement and is therefore subject to payment of listing commission whether it be sold before or after termination of employment.

It is also a good idea to include a specific period of notice in the contract in the event that either party (broker or sales agent) wishes to terminate the employment agreement.

While you are talking about money with your interviewing broker, inquire about group medical insurance, disability insurance, and life insurance. Most small one-office firms will not be able to offer these benefits unless they are written as a part of the whole Realtor Board group. The large multi-office firms and sometimes the franchises do offer some types of programs. But don't expect to see the comprehensive and generous medical and dental care programs that are offered as benefits in the large corporations across the country.

ATMOSPHERE

Time and money are specifics and are usually negotiated in every office. Atmosphere is a more elusive quality, although I'm not sure it's very much less important. Office atmosphere can affect how comfortable and happy you are in your job every bit as much as your commissions and your working hours. How to judge it?

It would be easier for me to *show* you than to tell you. If we could walk together through some offices, we could talk about the feelings we were getting along the way. But we can't, so perhaps I can best advise you by saying that you are really the best judge of the best atmosphere for you, and suggesting that you become especially sensitive and responsive to your feelings as you tour your prospective offices.

Some questions to help you judge: Is the office super clean, sharp-edged, modern, and brightly lit? Is everything stacked symmetrically in its right and proper place? Or is there a sense of casualness, a kind of homey disarray? Is there more dust and disorder than you can accommodate to? Is it too dark, too cold? Or is there a formal kind of warmth, the way a house looks just *before* the guests arrive? Is there a coffee machine? And a place to sit near it? Do you hear the other agents talking among themselves? Do they welcome you with smiles, or do they stare at you suspiciously? Are there comfortable chairs or couches where prospective clients might sit? Is there a room large enough to hold a closing in? Are the desks arranged in rigid rows or creatively? Are the walls painted hard white with venetian blinds at the windows? Or are the colors soft with perhaps even some wallpaper here or there and complementary drapes at the windows? Are the floors carpeted? Tastefully? And most important of all, would *you* like to bring a customer to this office and would *you* like to spend a good part of each week in it?

GETTING A DESK

Let's assume you have chosen an office. Or perhaps I should say you and a broker have chosen each other. What then? First, of course, you will be assigned a desk and introduced to your fellow workers. Then you will begin the work of beginning, some of which will cost you money.

You have undoubtedly already paid the fees involved in getting your state license; now if your broker is a Realtor, you will need to join the National Association of Realtors, your state Realtor Association, and your local Board of Realtors. These dues are usually paid annually at a specified time each year, but as a new member, you will have to pay the fee when you join. In some areas it is pro-rated according to the time remaining before the next annual dues-paying date. If your broker is a franchise member, there may also be a small fee to join the franchise officially.

Are you feeling overwhelmed? Try to relax, there's more! Many brokers require their sales agents to pay for their own business cards (which you should order immediately), and many require that sales agents pay the local Multiple Listing Service for the sales agent's individual subscription to the listing sheets or listing books. You also need to check with your personal insurance agent to be certain that your car insurance covers business use since you will be driving potential buyers from house to house. And you will need to buy a good pocket-sized appointment book, a battery-operated calculator (several companies manufacture models specifically designed to figure interest rates and other real estate related calculations), and a briefcase. You can bring a coffee mug from home, a cushion for your chair, and perhaps a plant or two or some framed photos for your desk. And then it's you! You are a real estate agent, a member of the firm.

Your work begins with getting to know that firm. Many brokers assign a new agent to work alongside an experienced agent for a period of time, and although this means a good deal of running without pay, it is excellent training. You should also go out and personally inspect every listing that your office holds so that you will know what each house being advertised really looks like.

During your first week or two, take home two or three copies of every blank form in the office cabinet (you'll find offer forms, contracts, listing forms, renewal forms, reports of sale, price reduction forms, and lots more) and practice filling them out. When you think you have them right, ask your broker or office manager to go over them with you and then keep one correctly completed copy of each form in your briefcase as a model. (You'll be surprised at how very often you'll have to fill out forms when there is absolutely no one around to help.)

And last, but certainly not least in importance, begin to familiarize yourself with the format of the Multiple Listing Service listing sheets that you will be working with. You should be able to locate information on those sheets quickly whenever a buyer asks a question, and you can only do that with practice. Practice by taking several sample sheets and having friends or family members ask you questions about the houses described on them. After a while you'll know exactly where to look to find the amount of taxes on the property, or the cost of heating for the previous year, or the number of bathrooms, or the size of the lot, etc. etc.

And now you have finished getting started, and are ready to move ahead!

SIX

Selling Good Service

"THEY also serve who only stand and wait." The line from John Milton's sonnet *On His Blindness* still echoes occasionally against the walls of our departmentalized, computerized, high speed world. To my mind, it should be stamped in gold on the binding of every real estate salesperson's listing book.

Does that statement puzzle you? Does it sound as though I'm contradicting myself? After all, I'm the one who said a real estate saleswoman should be assertive, aggressive, competitive, energetic, active, self-starting, etc. etc. And yes, she should, but she should also serve by *standing and waiting.* Call it a paradox, if you like. Or call it counterpoint: two voices of music, each different, but worked together against each other and in support of each other in such a way that the performance is complex and simple at the same moment, and so beautiful. The counterpoint of aggressive, creative sales work and the patience to stand and wait is an essential element in the art of good service as a real estate professional in your community.

"Nice sounding theory," you say, "but what exactly do you mean?"

Let me begin by showing you *exactly* what I *don't* mean. In *The Complete Book of Home Buying* (published by Dow Jones) Michael Sumichrast and Ronald Shafer quote a wonderful example of people manipulation from the Champions Unlimited series of real estate lectures which is given by Tom Hopkins. The setting is a real estate office. The characters are a house-hunting couple and the Champion agent. This is the action as directed by Mr. Hopkins:

So, they're going ahead with you, now. You're excited, but suddenly they stop you. Suddenly, they say to you, "Well, Tom, we just don't jump into things. You know, we've always been the type that kind of like to sleep on it." Smile when they say that and say, "I can understand you wanting to possibly wait. I've been in this situation numerous times, and that's why I sit here, feeling the excitement that you both have for the home, I feel an obligation to try and help you get it. The other night I was reading about a man that we Americans have long considered one of our wisest men, Benjamin Franklin. Whenever ol' Ben found himself in a situation such as you're in today . . . Here's what ol' Ben used to do. He'd take a plain, white piece of paper. He'd draw a line down the middle and on this side (pointing to the left), he'd write 'yes' and he'd list all the reasons favoring his decision today. On the other side, all the reasons against it. Then, he simply counted up the columns and his answer was made for him. Why don't we give it a try, just to see what happens? If it's good enough for ol' Ben, it might be good enough for us, don't you think?" Then I want you to take and turn that piece of paper around, hand him the pen and say, "Help me, John, if you will. Let's just put x's for the yeses. Mary, you mentioned the neighborhood, didn't you? Put an x, John. And of course the landscaping, John. Then, of course, the fireplace. You were excited with the spacious living room, weren't you? Something I think is important is the street lights out front for the kids at night. The carpeting and draperies are custom quality. Remember out in the covered patio? You'd better put that down. Of course, the fence-enclosed rear yard. You'd better make an x there. Also, the location of the home itself. Can you think of any more? Well, then let's see how many reasons you can come up with against the decision." Now you shut up. You give them all the help you can on the yeses, and you let them take care of the noes. I have yet to have a person come up with more than two or three on the no side.

If you pour it on, you can go right through the home and tell them all the things that you tied them down on, then after they've pondered a while, put down a couple of things, then smile and say, "Well, let's see what we do have. Well, one, two, three, four, five, six, seven, eight, nine, ten, eleven, twelve, thirteen, fourteen, fifteen, sixteen, seventeen, eighteen. Well, that's eighteen on the "yes" side. Let's see the "no" side. That's three: don't you think the answer is really pretty obvious, John?" That's a major close.

But Sumichrast and Shafer advise the home buyer, "Before *you* sign on the dotted line, make sure you are investing *your* money in the home *you* want" (pp. 148-149, 1980 edition). And I advise *you* as a responsible sales agent to make sure *also* that those buyers *are sure.*

The kind of riding-the-crest-of-a-wave "major close" that Mr. Hopkins advocates often results in messy deals where the buyers want to pull out after the contracts are signed, and lawyers get involved in trying to find ways to get them out, and sellers get downright furious at the buyers, the lawyers, you, your agency, and real estate agents in general. And yes, maybe there will be no way out for those buyers and maybe your "major close" will bring you the commission on that deal. *But you will certainly never get a referral from any person involved in that sale.* So you make a deal and probably cut away half a dozen others over the next several years. It's more than a "major close," it's a slammed door to future success (and perhaps even to the serenity of your night's sleep).

Real estate sales is a business that builds upon itself. The warm handshakes at the closing and the words, "Thanks, Carolyn, you did a really great job!" are nontaxable earned income and very valuable. Besides bolstering your sense of self-worth, those words usually mean that new customers and clients will be coming your way by referral, and referred buyers and sellers are the most loyal of all.

If I were to rewrite Mr. Hopkins' scenario with the concept of professional service in mind, it would go like this:

> Suddenly, they say to you, "Well, Carolyn, we just don't jump into things. You know we've always been the type that kind of like to sleep on it." You smile and say, "I think that's a great idea. The end of a long day's house hunting is no time to make an important decision. I do think this is a great house for you, and I do think it will prove to be a good investment, but it's much more important that *you* think so, too. So take some time to really work through your thoughts and feelings. In fact, let me make a couple of suggestions to you that have worked for some other people.
>
> "Don't take the listing sheet on this house home with you

tonight. Instead, go back to your apartment, relax, have dinner, and then try on the house as you might try on a good suit that you want to get a lot of wear from. *And* since you both don't wear the same clothes, each of you should try on this house, *separately.* Let me tell you how.

"Each take a few sheets of paper and a pencil and go into separate rooms. Allow twenty minutes or more before you get together again. Then each of you try to draw the floor plan of that house from memory. Be sure you put in stairs, doorways, windows, kitchen appliances, everything you can think of. When you have finished drawing, try to imagine yourself living in the house you have drawn. Think of yourself getting up in the morning: How many people in which bathrooms at what time? What does the kitchen feel like at breakfast? Where do you have your coat hanging when you are about to go out for the day? How will you bring groceries into the house? Where will the children play when you are preparing dinner? Imagine a Thanksgiving dinner, a cocktail party, a barbecue. And as you try on your house, write down any questions that come into your mind alongside your floor-plan sketch.

"When the twenty minutes are up, get back together again and compare your floor plans. Now don't have an argument (smile): the floor plans will probably be different, and it doesn't matter who's right. The idea of this exercise is to become aware of how well you really do know this house and how well it really does suit your needs and your life-style.

"Then talk about it. Talk about what doesn't gibe on the two floor plans. Talk about what you like. Talk about the questions you noted as you tried the house on.

"If you still love the house and want it in the morning, call me and I'll make an appointment to go back with you. Then you can correct your floor plans and be sure you'll be comfortable in the house *before* you commit yourselves and your money. And as a bonus, I'll have a little time tonight to dig out the listings on some comparable houses that have sold in the area during the past year. We'll go through those and establish the limits of the ball park in which the price should fall. That will make the negotiating much easier and you'll feel more confident that this is a good investment as well as a good home." And then you escort your customers to the door.

Now I know you're thinking, "That's not a major close, it's a ten-beat rest!" and I can hear my critics saying, "She's not selling at all. She's just *standing* around and *waiting* for the house to sell itself." Yes, exactly. Good service is providing access to all available properties within a prospective buyer's price range, providing accurate and comprehensive information on these properties, sharing your professional knowledge and judgment, and then having enough respect for your customers as individuals to stand back and wait while they use *their* intelligence and judgment to make a major decision in *their* lives.

Some brokers and sales agents interested in quick volume business will say that my approach is too passive, that I have emasculated the selling process. They will say, "That's a woman talking. *She* doesn't have to keep a business going. The technique is entirely and typically feminine!" A prejudiced view? Yes, but attitudes that humanity spent centuries in forging won't dissipate in a decade. And I strongly disagree that the technique is feminine, and much prefer to call an approach that respects judgment without the use of emotional "hype" or time pressure, *humanistic.*

Also, contrary to the quick-signature critics' opinion, this process of sending buyers away to weigh and consider is *good* business procedure. In doing so you give the customers time, tools, and advice which they appreçiate, and at the same time, you set up a situation that leads them back to your desk. If they are still interested in that particular house after mentally testing it, they will call back and be on their way to a much stronger and more positive offer. If on the other hand they change their minds about the house, they do not have to handle the embarrassment of backing out of a deal and therefore can continue to work with you with pride and commitment.

Business based on volume alone is fine if you're hawking hot dogs at a baseball game, but as a real estate professional, you want *good* business. Initial or immediate volume is only a small part of that. So learn that standing and waiting is a part of service. And never push.

Never push, however, does not mean never lend a hand in assistance or never give advice. You may be selling a concrete entity—a house—but you are being paid your commission not for the house but for your professional service as the agent handling the house on the seller's behalf. Your goal therefore is to sell by providing good service. To help you get started toward the goal of providing the best possible service, I'd like now to look beyond the patience and respect aspect of service to its two other components: knowledge and efficiency. What can and should you as a real estate agent provide in each category?

KNOW THE COMMUNITIES IN WHICH YOU WORK

When I was a very green agent, I once drove a customer to a town twenty-five miles away to find a house that, on the listing sheet, looked perfect for him and was relatively inexpensive too. When we finally found our way to the address (I at the wheel, he directing from the street maps), we discovered that the house was indeed as attractive as its picture promised, but that the property was adjacent to a cottage colony motel that had long ago shut down. Most of the windows in the large main building of that motel were broken or boarded up, a few of the outermost cottages were occupied by month-to-month tenants, weeds were growing rampant everywhere, trash and empty bottles were scattered about, and several old cars and a washing machine stood rusting in the center courtyard like perversely humorous contemporary sculptures. Located next door to such a disaster no house would be a good investment. We had driven forty minutes on the promise of a listing sheet, and I was center stage with egg on my face.

It was a good lesson and I learned it permanently: *Real estate is a local business.* In order to serve your customers and clients well, you must know the area in which you work, and you must know the limitations of your knowledge. Don't try to sell or list in areas that are just names on a map to you. Refer your potential customers for those distant areas to an agent who can give them the service they are paying for, collect your referral fee, and spend your time where it will be most productive.

Become an expert on the communities you *can* adequately serve. Know tax rates and zoning ordinances, and master plans for future development. Get specific information on the programs offered in the schools of each town. Find out about parks, recreation services, garbage disposal, sewage treatment, water supplies, fire protection, police, ambulance and rescue squads, medical services, churches, banks, shopping centers, libraries, museums, restaurants, theaters, hobby groups, *everything.* Read the local papers carefully, and know what is happening in each town. Get to know the character of specific neighborhoods, even the names of important people in Little League, or Girl Scouts, or the Garden Club, or Newcomers' Club.

Keep your information on index cards in a file box on your desk. When you read about a new officer installed in an important group or an article about a new program for senior citizens sponsored by the YMCA, take a second to make a note of it on the card for that group, or put the clipping in the file box. Yes, you'll have to go through and clean the box out every once in a while, but from time to time there are slow days that drag by in this business, and your community file update might just help those hours pass. It will also help you sell houses.

When people buy a house, they also buy into a town, and a neighborhood. Your information will be appreciated, just as a formal introduction to a "right" person is appreciated. And if you are tactful, you can even use your file box as a listing tool, taking it along to demonstrate to potential sellers how well you know their community and therefore how well you can sell the location of their house as well as the house itself.

KNOW RELATIVE PROPERTY VALUE

Take two split-level houses. They have the same floor plan, and were built by the same builder, with the same extras. They are just about the same age and are in the same town. They are located on different streets, however, at opposite ends of the town. One sells for $5,000 more than the other.

As a responsible agent you must know why. You must have the answers to your customers' questions about what makes one neighborhood or town more desirable than another. Differences in value based upon location are *a priori* truth in the real estate business, but acquiring the ability to explain why will take some studying on your part. And sometimes you will find even then that the answers are elusive and complex.

Perhaps the best place to begin developing a concept of relative property value is your office comparables file. Within a short time and with little effort, your exploration of the file will shed light on sale price patterns, which areas sell high and which areas sell low.

The study of comparables will help you develop a sense of where property values differ and by how much, but you still must answer the question why, and that will depend on your perception, and your research and knowledge. It takes time. I suggest that you begin by choosing one area at a time. Drive out to it, alone. Look about as though you were investing your money there. What are the pluses and the minuses of the neighborhood, the land, and the town? Take notes. Choose another, different, area a few days later.

After you become familiar with a good many different neighborhoods that you serve, visit the planning board or zoning office of each town. Look carefully at their maps. Check for zoning changes, transition zones, open spaces, proposed highways, industrial complexes, high density housing areas, least cost housing allotments, shopping centers, and special projects such as municipal swimming pools or recreation complexes. The future as well as the past and the present affect the value of property.

While discussing relative property values, I must add a word of caution to you about the use of your professional knowledge. Just about every state now has laws against "blockbusting": the procedure of attempting to get listings or sell property because of the threat of changes in the racial or ethnic character of a neighborhood. For example, you must *never* approach a homeowner with remarks such as: "I just heard that the house next door was sold to blacks, or Chinese, or Chicanos, or Martians. Would you like to put your house on the market now before they move in and lower the property values in the neighborhood?" *That* is blockbusting and an ethical and legal offense serious enough to cause loss of your license in most states.

But how about less obvious situations? What do you say when a buyer asks, "Is this a racially mixed neighborhood?" or "Are there a lot of Jews around here?" or "I heard half of this town is Polish and Italian, is that true?"

These questions disclose the fears and prejudices of the people who ask them, and whether we like it or not, the prejudices do exist in this country. They also put the agent committed to fair housing practices in a tight position. I advise you to answer the questions as honestly and factually as you can, with statistics if you have them, and without any emotional or prejudicial overtones as to how the answers affect property value.

If your buyers or sellers press you with questions like: "How does the racial and ethnic makeup of this town affect its property value now? Or in the future?" discuss the *factual* information that you have gathered on relative property value with them. Show them comparables, discuss the relative merits of school systems, taxes, recreation programs, tell them which towns and neighborhoods sell at higher prices and faster or at lower prices and slower, but do *not* become involved in their particular emotional attitudes about social and ethnic demographics. If you are pressed for more information or for your personal opinion, make a statement such as: "As a real estate professional, I can provide you with factual information on property values in these towns (areas). You are asking, however, for an opinion—not only my opinion but also my opinion of what other people will think and feel. I can't give you that because opinions are different for each individual who looks at a piece of property. You have the right and responsibility to make your judgment on a piece of property based on the factual information available and upon what you see and feel. No one can do this for you."

I strongly believe it is the responsibility of real estate agents to act as fairly and impartially as humanly possible, but remember buying or selling a home is an emotional process as well as a financial one and you are going to come up against emotional responses during your career. If you would like more information on fair housing, you can write for a copy of the Federal Fair Housing Act of 1968 from:

Office of Public Information
Department of Housing and Urban Development
451 7th Street N.W.
Washington, D.C. 20024

KNOW WHAT MAKES A "GOOD" HOUSE

Nationally, recent statistics from moving companies indicate that one family in five moves in any given year and statistics from lending institutions indicate that the majority of mortgages are paid off by the sale of the property within seven years. Today, therefore, buying a house or condo is both buying a home and buying an investment. A good agent should be able to point out to customers the features in a piece of property that make for good living, low maintenance costs, and good potential resale.

We've just discussed the importance of location in determining property value, so let's look here at the house itself, its structure and physical condition, its traffic pattern or floor plan, its amenities, and its lot and siting.

Physical condition and structure are probably easiest to discuss because the standards are more or less universal. Does the roof leak? Are termites eating away at it? Has the foundation cracked from uneven settling? How good is the insulation? Is there water in the basement? You will eventually be asked all of these questions and you should be able to give at least some information in your answer. You must also be ready and able, however, to recommend competent house inspection services, or private contractors to examine a particular problem, for you cannot forget that no matter how many wet basements you see, you are *not* a professional waterproofer.

I strongly recommend that as you begin showing houses you also spend some time reading some of the how-to-buy-houses books on the market and in libraries. Almost all of them have a chapter or two on construction and maintenance which will help you to become aware of potential trouble spots. Your best assistance to customers regarding structural or maintenance problems, however, is not your evaluation of how serious the problem is or how much it will cost to repair, but your professional evaluation of how important the problem is as a selling drawback in your area. For example, water in the basement is an absolute turn off in some areas, whereas sump pumps are so common in other areas that customers are surprised when they don't see one. It takes time (working time) to develop a sense of what's important where, but just being aware that you are seeking this kind of knowledge will help you to acquire it.

A sense of "good" floor plan also develops over time, but it is complicated by being tied to individual family needs and life-style and to what is fashionable at a given time and in a given local area. Currently, throughout the United States, the kitchen is the most important room in the house, and bright and big is very much "in." One and a half baths minimum is becoming a *must,* and basement family rooms are "out." Traffic patterns that lead through one room in order to reach another have always been detrimental to a sale, although the kitchen seems to be an exception to this rule. Everyone seems to expect to walk through the kitchen.

The current desirability or detriment of other features is influenced more by geographical location. In some parts of the country, basements are a must; in others most houses are built on slabs. The East Coast seems to prefer separate dining rooms, the West, large open areas that can be living and dining room combinations. Swimming pools are a high priority item in the South; they are sometimes an actual detriment to a sale in the North. Two-story structures called "colonials" are the hottest thing on the market in some parts of the country; other parts favor one-story construction which they call "ranches" or "contemporaries." Smaller houses, semi-attached houses, and high-rise condos seem to be taking over the market in many areas, yet others still hold out for elegance, privacy, and open land.

Watch for trends in your working area. The real estate section of the newspaper can be a help. What is being advertised most? What features headline display ads? Also talk with the other agents in your office and try to get a sense of what each of them would mention as a selling feature and why.

The size and contour of an individual lot and the siting of a house on its lot are also sales features strongly influenced by geographical and regional factors. In northern parts of our country, many energy-wise home buyers put a premium on houses with a majority of window areas facing south and shaded in summer; whereas in the South, northern light is preferred. In hilly areas, lots on the up-side of a road are usually more in demand. In flat areas, rectangular and regular lots are much preferred to oddly shaped pieces of property. Heavily wooded is a plus to some buyers in some areas, an impossibility in other parts of the country. Small lots are not only acceptable, but desirable in most urban areas; they are often hard to sell in rural areas. Obviously, it all depends, and you must find out what's valuable in your particular area.

KNOW YOUR CUSTOMERS AND CLIENTS

Forgive the generalization, but engineers do not make good real estate agents. The kind of person who is attracted to a career in engineering likes equations to work out, materials to bear predictable amounts of stress, and time and task to fit together. In real estate nothing equates neatly to anything else because "x" is always variable; lots of things break down when they're least supposed to; and no amount of planning can ensure that anyone or anything will be anywhere at a particular time. People who like very clear lines and crisp edges usually drop out of the real estate game.

Most successful agents can stay loose enough to spend an extra fifteen or twenty minutes talking with a new listing client about family camping trips or pet cats, or can stop an afternoon's house hunting for a cup of coffee and some good conversation when spirits begin to droop. Getting to know people, their motivations, interests, hobbies, prejudices, plans and hopes for the future, their *individuality,* is one of the key factors in effective and professional service. Knowing your customers and your clients will help you to find the "right" house, or the "right" buyer, or the "right" price in many a deal. So stop to listen, and care.

KNOW THE MORTGAGE MARKET

Some larger real estate offices subscribe to computerized information services which provide each agent with a weekly update on mortgage rates and qualification requirements at every area lending institution. This makes life easier. In smaller offices or more rural areas, however, you must do the same work. Work in this case means weekly telephone calls to check with mortgage representatives. It doesn't take long, but it's a must, whether you are listing or selling.

You must also read. Research and become very familiar with all the various types of financing available in your area. Watch newspapers and financial magazines for forecasts of new trends in financing or new financing methods. In times of tight money, agents who really know the money market are the only ones who make sales.

KNOW THE LOCAL LAWYERS AND THE LAW

Closing procedures vary across the country. In some areas lawyers represent both parties at the closing table; in other areas the financial institution handles the closing; and in still other areas there are closing specialists who oversee the transaction. Find out the procedure in your state and/or county. In fact, ask more experienced agents if you may accompany them to their closings, and watch. Begin to gather a reference list of the names of people involved in closings whom you consider efficient and competent. A day will come when you will need that list.

And keep the manuals and textbooks you used in studying for your state real estate exam. I assure you, sometime within your first year you will need to return to them to check a point of real estate law or a puzzling term.

In reading all this, I hope it's obvious to you that I'm not advocating a crash course in "knowledge." As in every other profession, real estate knowledge comes with both study and experience. Yours will grow more quickly, however, if you are aware of your objectives and if you remain receptive to and aware of the knowledge that is gained in the experiences of each working day.

And now to efficiency. I said just a bit ago that engineers, who are some of the world's most efficient people, make poor real estate agents for the very reason that they want and try to run things both efficiently and on time. "How can that be bad?" you ask. Well, look at the real estate game. How can anyone be efficient when customers don't show up or show up forty-five minutes late for an appointment? When sellers lock their storm doors so that you can't use the key box? When buyers insist on stopping after the third house on a list of five because they like it and want to think over buying it, leaving you with two infuriated sellers who rate you as a "no show"? When other agents forget to report a sale? When the MLS fails to publicize a price reduction? When the newspaper prints the wrong phone number on your feature ad? Or when two feet of snow fall the day your transfer family from Arizona arrives in town? Need I go on?

There is no way you will always appear efficient and in control if you work in a business so continually dependent upon the activity and action of other people. The real trick of survival, however, is to learn to avoid as many of the slippery banana peels in your path as you can. The following are but suggestions gleaned from my own experience to help you maintain your efficiency as well as the appearance of it.

KEEP YOUR LISTINGS UP TO DATE

This often requires time and a fussy kind of busy-work that many agents resent. But keep in mind an agent who rang the bell to show a house only to be told angrily by the person who answered the door that the house had been sold, closed, and moved into by the new owners!

TAKE LISTINGS CAREFULLY

Before sending listing information to the MLS board, check the tax figures and lot dimensions that the owners gave you. You can call the tax collector's office for the tax information and try to obtain a copy of a survey or an old plat plan for the lot dimensions. Also measure every room and include the dimensions on your listing sheet. Doublecheck phone numbers, the spelling of names, and the list of personal items such as drapes, appliances, and lawn furniture which are included in the asking price of the house, and those that are not. Check to be sure your listing contract has an expiration date, and be sure your sellers understand the commission agreement.

PLAN SHOWING ROUTES CAREFULLY

Plot your course on a local street map before your customers arrive. If possible drive it and pre-inspect each house. Don't let yourself be caught looking foolish by getting lost in the middle of a maze-like development.

ALLOW ENOUGH TIME

This means allow more time than you think you'll need. Just about everything in this world takes longer to do than we think it should. It's better to stop for coffee, to take up slack time, than to arrive at each house on your list later and later, or to rush your buyers through a house they seem to like because the next seller is expecting them in five minutes and is located thirty minutes across town.

KEEP AN ACCURATE POCKET DATEBOOK WITH YOU AT ALL TIMES

Does this need explanation?

FOLLOW UP ON ALL PAPERWORK

Assume nothing. If possible hand deliver contracts or any other papers that are time sensitive. Keep checking with the banks on mortgage applications. Add and re-add figures on contracts. Draw up a checklist for both buyers and sellers titled "What to do before closing." These lists should include such items as "have electric meter read," "have oil in tank measured," "bring certified check for x dollars to the closing," "bring a copy of insurance policy to closing."

And keep copies of everything—everything, every letter, signed document, phone message, request for information or service—*everything,* in your own personal "Transaction Pending" file. Most of the time you will not need any of this information, but when and if you do, it can be extremely hard to come by.

APOLOGIZE FOR INCONVENIENCE OR MISTAKES

No matter how you try, you will occasionally be late for appointments, or not be able to show up at all. Or take the wrong road and end up five miles out of town with a customer who needs to catch a plane. Or something else. Learn to say "I'm sorry" sincerely. There is no other remedy.

Despite all this good advice (and even if you were to adhere to every word of it), you will undoubtedly lose some customers during your career and you will probably make some angry. You will feel bad and probably wonder what you could have done to make the situation work out better. Try not to spend too much time or energy on the wondering and worrying. Maybe there is no answer or maybe the answer is "nothing." Nothing could have made your deal work. When you've tried your hardest and everything has fallen apart, remember this slight distortion of a famous quotation from Lincoln: "You may *satisfy* all of the people some of the time; you may even *satisfy* some of the people all of the time; but you can't *satisfy* all of the people all the time."

SEVEN

The Listing Farm

AT THE risk of sounding like a second-grade teacher, I'd like to ask you to play a game with me, an imagining game. Pretend, if you will, that you are a homesteader on the Great Plains in the mid-nineteenth century. You and your husband have found a site that suits you and have staked out your claim with the government. Now you must build a house and a barn and break up the earth into the fields and furrows of a farm. The work, the demands, the pressures seem endless. Always there is some new tool, or seed, or stock to be bought, some additional shelter or fence to be built, some crop or animal to be tended. Your hours are long, your expenses high; yet at the end of your first year, your financial yield is small.

As October of your second year approaches, your life seems less frantic to you, your body aches less, and sometimes you can stay awake later into the evening to read, or knit, or talk with a friend. The second harvest is good. There is enough money for some extras and enough time to expand your farm by opening two new fields.

By the end of your third year, you find life comfortable, almost secure. There is a rhythm in the seasons and in the kinds of time and energy they demand, and there is a rhythm in each day. Sometimes the beat is quick and light, sometimes slow and steady, yet within each different pattern you have also found the rests. When the rhythms are disrupted, when the droughts and fires and emotional crises of every life break upon you, you work harder again to survive and then you re-establish the old rhythms or become accustomed to new ones in order to keep your farm productive.

"A nice bit of imagination, almost poetic," you say to me, "but why are you including a homesteading saga in a book about how to be a real estate agent?"

Well, it's too short for a saga, really. Think of it as a fable or a parable, a story that has a message, a story in which the characters and events represent something more than what they appear to be. The pioneer farm woman is you, the beginning real estate agent. Her homestead is your real estate listing farm.

"Farming" in real estate trade jargon means working on the listing end of the business. Like many jargon words, it has been appropriated into real estate from another trade because of multiple similarities. Listing for the real estate agent, like working the fields for the farmer, provides the raw material, the products that can be sold at market to make a living. Without earth and seed, sun and water, there is no produce; without listings, there is no real estate business.

Establishing your listing farm, like establishing a homestead in the nineteenth century, is often a time-consuming and tiring process in the early years. The hours and energy spent, however, usually increase the yield of each succeeding year, which means of course increasing financial rewards. If you take the time to establish and care for a good listing farm, you will survive the droughts and fires (the recessions and interest rate fluctuations) on that farm, which is of course your whole career.

"Establish" and "care for." Exactly how does one establish and care for a listing farm? The "establish" part is finding the earth and the tools to work it; the "care for" part is doing the work. Let's look at listing tools first; then we'll survey the earth; and finally we'll discuss methods of farming.

YOU AND YOUR PERSONALITY

There is no farm without a farmer, and a listing farmer to a great degree determines her own success. Goal setting, determination, time management, perseverance, knowledge, ability, planning, and sometimes (to borrow a word from the Yiddish language) a little *chutzpah* all contribute to success.

But there are other factors, too. Your appearance, for example. Do you look professional, competent, neat, successful? No one wants to entrust the sale of his property to a disheveled, uncertain "has been" or "could be." People want the most for their money and, in hiring a real estate agent, they want someone who has been successful and will continue to be successful. So even if you have never made a sale and are knocking on the first door of your listing farm, *look* successful. If necessary, invest some money in a fine quality suit and good shoes, even if you must wear the same clothes with minor variations almost every day until the first commission check arrives. The investment will pay off.

If your office is a franchise member, the question of attire may have a predetermined answer. Many franchises now require uniforms for all sales agents, usually a blazer with the franchise emblem and slacks or a skirt. Some salespeople object, of course, but the franchise replies that market research has proven the importance of the salesperson's appearance relative to her success, and the franchise wants everyone to look well dressed and successful. (They also want their logo to appear around town as much as possible.)

After a prospective client opens the door and sees you, his or her next impression of you will be influenced by your voice and speech pattern. Above all, speak *clearly,* neither too loud nor too soft. And if you must choose, it is better to speak too slowly than too fast. In fact, studies have shown that people are not really aware of how fast they are speaking, especially when they are anxious or nervous. So think *"slowly"* to yourself as you speak, and you'll probably end up near normal.

Tone is also important and harder to pin down into "how-to." Try to keep your voice and manner warm and friendly, without being overpowering or gushy. Avoid, above all, projecting any hint of a "canned" (memorized) speech. Try to make the person who answers the door feel that you are sincerely interested in meeting him/her as an individual and that you have a genuine interest in his/her home and plans for moving either soon or in the distant future. This is sometimes difficult to carry through when it's your eleventh stop of the afternoon, but try, and if you can't keep your tone fresh and interested, it's time to stop for the day.

Also smile. It's amazing how much a smile will help.

YOUR AGENCY

The real estate laws of every state prohibit licensed salespersons from acting as an agent in any real estate transaction except while in the employ of a licensed broker. A salesperson cannot place an advertisement in the newspaper under her own name; she cannot place a for sale sign on a piece of property unless it bears her agency name, and she cannot even show a house except as the representative of the broker who employs her.

The agency in which you choose to hang your license therefore is a very important part of the development of your career. As you begin your listing farming, one of your primary tools will be telling prospective clients the services your agency offers and how and why it will best handle the particular piece of property they want to sell.

In the large multi-office companies and in the franchise member offices, the storage closets are full of listing crutches. There are introduction mailings, and search mailings, and new neighbor mailings, and there are give-aways such as pot holders, jar openers, calendars, Frisbees, etc.; there are printed flyers of all kinds, and sample magazine and newspaper display ads, and video tapes and tape players that you can carry about with you; and sometimes even loose-leaf manuals which the agent is instructed to read aloud step-by-step while sitting in the living room with the prospective sellers.

In small independent firms, the responsibility for representing the agency falls much more heavily upon the talents of the individual agent, upon your ability to stand on your own two feet without crutches. You must be able to explain how the particular neighborhood location of your office is advantageous to those sellers; or the special care with which the advertising from your office is written; or your broker's willingness to show properties and handle time-sensitive situations when the listing agent is away from the office; or to give assistance when negotiations get tough; or the outstanding record of your office in arranging excellent financing. You will have to know the strengths of your firm and be able to judge which strengths will be most important and impressive to the particular sellers with whom you are talking. And then you must present those strengths effectively.

Describing the virtues of your agency (whether large or small) takes some practice and you probably won't win any awards for your first few performances. But the only way to improve is to do it.

One note of caution here: real estate laws in all states prohibit payment of commission or gratuities from a real estate transaction to any party not licensed as a broker or salesperson and directly involved in the transaction. There are also regulations prohibiting the use of certain give-aways, raffles, prizes, or other inducements to listing. It would take a great deal of space to discuss the minor differences in terminology and restrictions that exist from state to state, so I can only refer you to your own state law book and suggest that you think twice before making it your standard policy to invite to dinner at the most expensive restaurant in town every new seller who lists with you.

THE COMPETITIVE MARKET ANALYSIS

Some real estate tools have been around for a long, long time. The use of market sales data to help determine the fair market value of a property is one of the oldest, and still one of the most effective. It has just recently been named the competitive market analysis (and the name is sticking and spreading throughout the country with electronic speed due to the networking of the franchises and the giant firms). To my mind, it is one of the most important services a professional real estate agent can offer a prospective seller.

Briefly, a competitive market analysis is a comparison of the property which your clients hope to sell with similar properties in the same geographical area which have sold during the past six months to a year. By means of careful feature by feature comparison and discussion of location, age, amenities, motivations for selling, and local and national marketing and mortgaging conditions, you, the agent, help the sellers arrive at a realistic probable selling price and a realistic asking price.

Unfortunately, the practice is prohibited in Alabama by section 34-27-36 of the License Law (Act#422) which reads, "No real estate broker or real estate salesman licensed by the Alabama Real Estate Commission can advertise or offer in any manner free appraisals, market analysis, free home estimate, or neighborhood analysis." To my knowledge, market data evaluations are being practiced virtually everywhere else throughout the country. They are your best listing tool, and you should learn to do such evaluations of property value at the very beginning of your career.

To do a competitive market analysis (CMA), you make your appointment to visit the property when all the parties with a share in its ownership are present. If you have not made face-to-face contact with the owners or seen the property, ask the owners while you are on the phone about the style, size, age, number of bedrooms, and baths, and any special features in the house. Then, if possible, drive by the home yourself so that you can evaluate the lot, the location, and the exterior.

Once you are familiar with the house, search the comparables file (or the comparables computer print-out book) for every house in the immediate neighborhood that has sold during the past year. Then expand your search to houses of similar size, age, and style throughout the town or even the neighboring towns. You should have a minimum of six good comparables when you have completed your search, more if possible. If you cannot find six very similar properties, choose houses a little smaller or larger to compare to your potential listing.

A CMA is somewhat more difficult when you are evaluating an unusual house, such as a restored antique, or a converted carriage house, or an architect-designed contemporary, but in theory the process still works. You can compare the values of surrounding properties and of properties with the same interior living space in comparable locations. On these special houses, however, you may also wish to do a replacement cost analysis. Here you call a local reputable builder or two in order to ascertain the current dollar cost per square foot in building a new house. Then you measure the foundation, multiply it out to get the living space, and add the value of amenities, extras, special building materials, and the lot. Between the CMA and the replacement cost estimate, you and your clients should be able to arrive at a fairly accurate estimate of current value. And then, if your sellers are not under immediate pressure to sell, you can test your accuracy by putting the house on the market on the high side of your estimated value range.

When you arrive to do the CMA, make a careful tour of every room of the house including garage, basement, and attic. Listen to the owners as they tell you about their home and note *(write down)* all the special features. Then sit down in the living room before a coffee table, or preferably at the kitchen table with a cup of coffee if it is offered, and get out the comparables you chose. Give them to the owners to look at while you fill out the blank listing sheet that you have brought along with all the information on the house that you just toured. Note special features, extras included in the sale, taxes, lot size, heat, electrical service, sewerage, *everything.*

Then, when everyone is ready, begin a point by point comparison of the house you are in with the houses around it and similar to it that have sold in the past year. Discuss the asking prices on those other houses, the length of time they remained on the market, the price reductions, and the actual selling prices. Let your sellers express their opinions of where the house value should fall before you express yours, if you can. This will give you the opportunity to discuss positives and negatives in their estimates and then to present your own evaluation with documentation and comparisons.

After some experience doing CMAs, you should be able to hone in quite closely on the value of the house you are discussing, but it is usually wise to take a conservative approach and express your ideas by quoting a price range. For example, "I think the market value of your property is between $84,000 and $87,000, Mr. & Mrs. Seller." Then discuss the negotiating space prevalent in your area and suggest a good asking price. Again for example, "Most houses are now selling within 5 percent of the asking price in this area so I think a price tag of $91,500 would be a good place to start." (You make this calculation on your pocket calculator by dividing the top figure of your price range by .95 and then rounding off to the next lower 500.) You explain that this asking price allows them the possibility of getting even slightly more than your top estimate of $87,000, but it also allows room for a price reduction as a selling incentive or considerable room for negotiating down to $84,000 or $85,000, if the sale should go slowly.

If your sellers agree, it is a good idea to ask for the listing right then and there. Don't be upset, however, if their response is that they would like to sleep on it. Many sellers like to talk with several agents before listing and you should respect their caution as good business sense. Thank them for their time, tell them you'll get in touch with them in a day or two, and then leave with the assurance and good feeling that you have given it your best try. Don't forget to call them back, however; you are not bothering them, you are assuring them of your continued interest.

HAND TOOLS

Besides your self-assurance and professionalism, you must carry a few things with you in your briefcase or the glove compartment of your car. As I've already mentioned, a pocket calculator and completed copies of all office forms are a must. In addition, you need a fifty-foot retractable metal measuring tape to be used in measuring rooms, or the entire foundation when figuring square footage, or outside distances such as the setback from the road or the distance of the house from a stream that runs along the side of the property.

You need a good flashlight (be sure to keep the batteries fresh) to inspect basements, attics, the depths of closets, or any other place where lighting is poor. And do so carefully. You want to be sure that you have seen and understood the house as well as listened to the information given by the sellers, for you too can be held responsible for misinformation printed on a listing sheet which buyers accept as fact.

Slip a small magnet into your briefcase to test for cast iron pipes. Copper or plastic plumbing will not attract the magnet, cast iron will. (Generally you will find cast iron pipes only in older houses.) And take along a small pocketknife or ice pick to test the beams for termites if you suspect them. You also need a clipboard and paper to take notes and make calculations.

Do not hesitate to discuss problems you notice in a house with the sellers. For example, if the basement looks as though it gets flooded from time to time, ask them about it and tell them that almost everyone else (buyers, agents, home inspection services, bank appraisers) who inspects the house will have the same questions and doubts. It is better from both a marketing and negotiating point of view to explain and define unusual conditions at the outset.

You now have your tools; where do you farm?

YOUR NEIGHBORHOOD

The properties within a quarter mile radius of your home are your most fertile ground. Because you live in an area, you are *ipso facto* an expert on it. You are, in the image of your neighbors, "the neighborhood professional," the one who really knows property value. You should play upon the advantages of this image to the utmost. Get to know your neighbors.

First, have your office send out a flyer with your photo on it and a little biographical blurb announcing that you have joined the ABC Realty firm and will be representing it in your neighborhood. (That flyer can be printed at nominal cost by a local quick-print shop.) In a small office, you yourself will probably have to address the envelopes; in a large one you may have secretarial help.

Then, within the next few weeks, stop at every house to which the flyer was mailed and personally introduce yourself, point out where in the neighborhood you live, leave your business card, and offer a free competitive market analysis if the owner expresses any interest in knowing the current market value of his/her property.

Your geographical proximity to these people gives you a strong advantage over other agents, and the CMA you offer is an opportunity to get to know them better and earn their confidence in you as a professional. (It is also a chance for you to practice doing the CMA.)

If you have the time and inclination, and if your office is willing to support you, it is an excellent idea to put together a pamphlet or even a one-page flyer explaining competitive market analysis as a market data approach to determining the value of a home. You can then staple your card to the corner of the pamphlet and assure yourself a better chance of the card remaining about the house rather than being thrown in the trash.

For the pamphlet, I would suggest something like:

DO YOU KNOW WHAT YOUR HOUSE IS REALLY WORTH IN TODAY'S REAL ESTATE MARKET?

The ABC Realty Agency can help you find out
ABSOLUTELY FREE and
WITH ABSOLUTELY NO OBLIGATION

HERE'S HOW!

We'll make an appointment to come to your home at your convenience. After inspecting it carefully and discussing its special features with you, we will show you the listings of previously sold homes in your area and discuss with you the differences and similarities between those homes and yours. We will then examine the actual selling prices of those homes with you, their length of time on the market, and the amount of price reduction which resulted from negotiation. Comparing this information with our personal knowledge of your home, we will be able to give you an informed opinion of the fair market value of your property and suggest a competitive and attractive asking price.

CALL 555-1234.
OUR OFFICE IS OPEN SEVEN DAYS A WEEK

If you call on a neighborhood house and there is no one at home, leave the pamphlet and then call by phone later in the day. It's an excellent lead to say, "Did you get the pamphlet I left? What do you think of the market data approach? Would you like to have it done?"

You will get a lot of "No, not right nows" of course, but don't take them as personal rejections. Keep in touch with all of these neighborhood people. Once they begin to remember your name, you as a neighbor will have an excellent shot at their listing when they do think of moving. And they may even refer you to a friend or relative who wishes to move into the area.

YOUR TERRITORY

In large multi-office firms and in some franchised firms, your broker or office manager may assign you to a particular area or section of a town which will be your farming territory. You will be expected to work the area by becoming especially familiar with it and by canvassing. In other firms, you will be given free rein to do your farming wherever you choose. I advise you to choose areas as close to home as possible, but for your own purposes mark them out on a street map and seriously work them.

Once you step out beyond your immediate neighborhood, however, you are farming more difficult terrain. You have begun "cold canvassing." There are two kinds: door-to-door and phone. Both present problems, both need training and practice, and both can be very profitable. Let's start with door-to-door.

To pick a street in your territory and begin knocking on doors brings up some logistical and psychological problems. Rather than projecting the image of a neighbor introducing herself, you are now a stranger selling something. The homeowner's resistance to you is increased tenfold, with suspicion added as a bonus. On the other hand, your own psyche adds elements of fear and defensiveness to whatever resistance it already has to unfamiliar situations.

Starting is the hardest part. Most real estate training

programs recommend an approach something like this:

> *Ring bell.* Hello, I'm Ann Seller of ABC Realty. Have you heard of my office? (This question is included here to get the owner involved in the conversation and to give the sales agent a chance to tell him/her where the office is located.) *The agent continues*: We're making a door-to-door survey of this neighborhood because we have buyers who have expressed an interest in the area. You have a particularly (lovely, desirable, well-located, large, saleable, well-maintained, or whatever else you can think of to say about it) home. Do you have any plans to sell in the near future? *Response. If No*: Well, I certainly can't blame you. You must be very comfortable here and your home is definitely a very good investment that is growing in value all the time. But perhaps you can help us. Do you happen to know of anyone who *is* planning a move? *Response. Whether positive or negative reply*: Thank you very much for taking the time to talk with me today, Mrs. Homeowner. May I give you my card and this description of a free service we offer to help homeowners determine the current market value of their properties? *Offer the CMA flyer with the agent's card stapled to it. Follow up all leads on potential movers with personal calls as soon as possible.*
>
> *If response to "Do you have plans to sell?" is "Yes, eventually, but not for at least six months or a year"*: Well, Mrs. Homeowner, I'm sure you'll do very well in the real estate marketplace when you're ready to sell. We'd like very much to handle a property like this one professionally. I have a description here of a free service we offer that will help you determine the current market value of your home. *Offer the CMA flyer.* And I'm sure my agency can effectively market your property. I hope you'll call me if you have any real estate questions at all. *The agent should call these potential sellers from month to month to check on the status of their selling plans and try to establish a working rapport.*

When door-to-door canvassing brings you face to face with sellers who are indeed thinking of selling their home in the near future, offer to return that evening or at a time convenient to all the owners and do the CMA as a complimentary service. And then sell yourself and your agency.

As a woman, you have some advantages in door-to-door

canvassing, since you will primarily encounter other women in your daytime work. They will be less defensive toward you than toward a strange man. There is also some risk to the sales agent involved in door-to-door work, however, and I recommend that all canvassing be done in pairs.

It is not a good idea, however, to approach individual homes together, since good selling is on a one-to-one basis and since the homeowner is always somewhat overwhelmed and more defensive when faced with a pair of agents. Instead, I suggest that you and your partner cover opposite sides of the street, or alternate houses, or opposite sides of a hallway in a high-rise condo complex. Keep loose tabs on each other's whereabouts and the time being spent in any particular dwelling. Difficulties in daytime door-to-door canvassing are rare, but knocking at the doors of strangers always involves some uncertainties, and having a partner who knows where you are and how long you've been there can eliminate some of your tension and also provide some relief from the tedium of the job. (Take a break or two for coffee.)

Don't expect to pick up half a dozen listings the day you go out cold canvassing. Really, this is seed sowing time. You are trying to introduce yourself and your agency, offer a service, and get leads on houses about to go on the market. But sometimes you will pick up a listing, and then you should definitely go out to dinner to celebrate!

If you are planting seeds when door-to-door canvassing, you are merely breaking ground and tilling when phone canvassing. Most training programs recommend that you make five cold canvass phone calls a day on a regular basis. When told this, most agents are a bit stunned, stare blankly, and then respond, "But what do I *say?*"

The standard canned speech goes like this:

> Good morning, Mrs. Housewife. This is Ann Seller of ABC Realty. How are you? *(pause)* I'm calling because our agency has customers particularly interested in your neighborhood and we are trying to locate homeowners who are planning to sell in the near future. Would you be able to help us out on this?

The philosophy behind this approach is to find the person who will say either "Well, we're not selling, but I heard Tom Jones on the corner was going to be transferred," or the person who will say, "Well, we've been thinking about selling for quite a while, but we don't see anything better around that we can afford." The first response should take you immediately to the door of Tom Jones; the second is a lead on both a listing and a potential sale.

If the cold canvass call draws a negative response, sales trainees are instructed to end the conversation positively:

> Thank you for talking with us, Mrs. Housewife. I'd like to send you a brochure about our firm and/or about real estate values in this area, and/or (anything your office has available) as a token of my appreciation. And if you ever have a real estate question, please don't hesitate to call me. There's never any charge or obligation.

Then send the material with your card attached.

One instructor teaching a class that I attended seemed to be finishing up his bit on phone canvassing when he turned suddenly toward us, pointed a finger at a student and said, "Why the hell do you think we go through this shit with the phones?" The poor woman was startled speechless. The instructor drew back a bit, but he continued to pose the question to almost everyone in the room. He elicited the standard answers: to get listings; to get leads; to get contacts for the future. "All possibilities," he said, "but you're all wrong. The reason, the real reason, that we want you to make five phone calls a day is to find the neighborhood busybody. Then you make friends with her. You call her and chew the fat every two weeks or so. She is your bird dog. *She's* the one who'll tell you where the listings are before they're there!"

I remember resenting this man's attitude and his obvious put-down of housewives as gossips with nothing better to do but "chew the fat" on the phone. And I think the odds of finding such a person and actually becoming friends over the phone are on the long side of ridiculous.

In fact, I feel that cold phone canvassing (the kind where you pick five names at random from the phone book) is a rude intrusion on the people being called. Perhaps door-to-door canvassing is an intrusion also, but at least the agent is visiting the neighborhood and becoming acquainted with the individual houses and their occupants. The phone call is a blind, impersonal break in someone's day.

Many times I have been startled in the middle of composing a sentence, or have come running up from doing laundry in the basement to answer a call that went, "Good morning! This is Giant Catalogue Stores calling. Would you like to buy any of our panty hose special today?" I am usually irate enough to slam the phone down without response, and I certainly can't in good conscience recommend such an intrusion as a part of a professional real estate sales program.

There is a kind of phone canvassing I do recommend, however. Perhaps you could call it warm phone canvassing. It is done from your personal card file that you build up as you work in the profession. Five phone calls a day *are* a good idea, but they should be to old customers, business acquaintances, people you meet while door-to-door canvassing, neighbors, friends, lawyers, bankers, relatives, anyone you know but haven't talked with in a while. And there is *no* canned speech that works or should work. The purpose of your call is to touch and keep contact. Ask how things are going and remind the person that you are working in real estate and seeking listings. Make your calls friendly but short. The time will be well spent and rewarding. (It is certainly easier to till and plant a field that you worked a year or two ago than to break new ground.) And besides, there is a certain joy, a lift to your day and his or hers when you talk with an established friend or acquaintance.

HOMEOWNER ADS

Many experienced sales agents believe that the most fertile farming soil for listings is advertised each week in the local newspaper classified ads. In fact, they maintain (and rightly so) that the advertisements are for more than good soil, they are actually advertisements for a crop ready to be harvested by an alert and competent agent.

Several years ago friends of ours put an ad in the local paper reading: "Three-bedroom ranch, 1½ baths, eat-in kitchen, family room, 1-car garage. $63,900. PRINCIPALS ONLY. 555-7891."

They received fourteen calls the first day. Eleven (!) were from real estate agents who wanted the listing. My friends had certainly paid for two unnecessary words: *principals only*. No one believed them. Their house was in a very saleable town and in a very saleable price range. Every top agent on the MLS board wanted a chance to bring it into his or her office. And within ten days, someone did.

There's a well-worn adage in the business that every "For Sale By Owner" ad is written by a seller in search of a listing broker. And the fact is that 90 percent of all houses sold in the United States are sold through real estate agents. Most homeowners do not know enough about marketing and legal procedures to effectively handle their own houses, and most of them are so emotionally involved in the process of selling their home that they overprice by many thousands of dollars. The result is that after a few weeks of frustration and rejection by potential buyers, they are ready to wash their hands of the chore and sign with a real estate firm. All of which explains the eleven agent calls out of fourteen, and underscores the belief that farming should be done aggressively in the newspaper.

Top agents call on homeowner ads the very first day they appear in the paper. But they don't try for the listing at that time, knowing that the phone is too busy and the seller too excited to be approached effectively. Instead these agents simply introduce themselves, mention their agency name, and state that they have customers seeking houses in the area where the sellers live. The agent then follows up her initial call with a mailing of some kind: the CMA flyer with a card attached would be a good example.

Perhaps three days later, the alert, aggressive agent will call again (by now the phone no longer rings constantly). She will ask the sellers if they received the printed material she sent and she will again express her interest in the property, perhaps mentioning that she drove by and was impressed by the exterior, or the lot, or the location. Tactfully, she will request a tour of the interior, perhaps suggesting that she might be able to give the sellers some marketing hints. While in the house, she will offer to return with comparables and do a CMA. If she has some buyers particularly suited to the property, she may even request a one-day written open listing to show them the house.

This procedure is an excellent path to new listings. Once you establish contact with a seller and visit the property that is for sale, you have the opportunity to break down many of the defensive barriers those sellers have erected against their stereotype image of real estate agents. You become a *person* to them and you have the chance to demonstrate your knowledge and efficiency in a highly technical and fast-moving profession. A good competitive market analysis done after the sellers have gone through three weeks of phone calls, and no-shows, and buyers without money, and lookers, and low-ball-offer artists, will increase your odds of landing the listing. A warm enthusiasm for the house as saleable, along with a bright description of your office will take you even further.

Of course your competition will be keen, and I repeat that you won't get every listing you try for, no matter how good you get. But if you try, you should get your fair share.

YOUR SPARE-TIME WORLD

Have you ever seen a Little League team in bright red jerseys with a local business name (Cozy Hearth Realty, for example) written across the front of each one? Their coach ordered three extra shirts in the adult size and wears them when he mows his lawn or runs to the corner store for milk. And yes, you guessed it, he's office manager for the Cozy Hearth Company in his town, and he's planning to coach again next year. He loves baseball, and kids (his own daughter is on the team), and he got three new listings in one spring season directly through his association with the local Little League.

Working your listing farm is a round-the-clock job; you are often working (planting seeds) when you think you are enjoying your time off. When the topic of least cost housing came up at your bridge club and you could speak knowledgeably about the zoning plans of the town, you impressed the opponent on your left. She calls you three months later because her husband is being transferred and they must sell their house. You pick up another listing from your co-chairperson of the PTA cake sale and get yet another from the cookie director for your daughter's Brownie troop.

Real estate, its values, selling procedures, and problems, are high interest topics of conversation in just about every community of every size across the country. As a professional in the field you will be listened to carefully when the topic comes up. Let people know you are a real estate agent and express your opinions, get into conversations, even disputes, and talk about your work, your agency, and what the future looks like to you. You never know when a well-placed word or two will bring a listing, or a lead, or a referral months later.

I guess just about everything in life overlaps somewhat. I promised to discuss the tools and earth of your listing farm, and in doing that I've talked a good deal about methods, too. But one very important method question still remains: *How does an agent actually get home sellers to sign a listing contract?* There's no one answer that works every time, but there are some positive steps that will increase your odds for success.

FILL OUT THE LISTING FORM

Do you remember that I suggested you fill out a blank listing form while your prospective sellers are examining the comparables you bring for the CMA? This thorough collection of information and your fussy care about getting all the facts down for comparison with other houses is not only a CMA tool, but also (and even more important) a listing tool. It is much easier to ask for signatures on a listing contract when all (or most) of the blanks on the property description section are already filled in. Minor details such as the exact size of the master bedroom or the amount of last year's heating bill can be added or amended later. What is important and impressive to the sellers is the amount of accurate information the real estate agency makes available to a prospective buyer.

Go over the property description with your sellers. Ask them if they can think of anything else that should be added, any feature that makes the house more desirable, and include their comments (within the limits that space permits) on the listing sheet.

Make your sellers feel important in their knowledge of their property, and be sure you let them know that you think their house is important, to you and to your agency. Nothing creates this impression as well as your very careful attention to detail.

EXPLAIN AGENCY RELATIONSHIP

This is the beginning of your real sales pitch for the listing. Somewhere in the course of your discussion (and you have to learn to get a feel for it; there's no universal right time) you must explain what it means to list with a real estate agency. For example, for an exclusive right to sell contract you might say: "During the time of your listing contract, Mr. & Mrs. Homeowner, the ABC Realty Company will be completely and exclusively responsible for the sale of your home. We as members of the Multiple Listing Service allow other members to show our properties in order to obtain the maximum exposure for you. But we will be a part of every negotiation and will be available to you for questions or services at all times."

For an exclusive agency listing, you might say: "In signing this listing contract, Mr. & Mrs. Homeowner, you give ABC Realty the exclusive right to act as your agents in the sale of your home. We will share the listing information and allow other members of the Multiple Listing Service to show your property in order to give your home the best and fastest chance to be sold. But we will be a part of all negotiations involving other agencies. In this type of contract, however, you as owners also reserve the right to sell your home yourself to a party that has *not* been introduced to you by an agency. If this occurs, you will owe no commission on the sale."

Many MLS boards will not accept exclusive agency listing, and if this is the case in your area, you must also explain to your sellers that in choosing the exclusive agency relationship over the exclusive right to sell they are cutting off the exposure of multiple listing. Some sellers prefer not to be included in the MLS listings, but they should understand that they can choose that option with either kind of listing.

In your explanation of agency relationship, you must also include information on exactly what services will be provided. Stress the importance of the third party (agent) in showing the home effectively without emotional involvement, in qualifying buyers as to their financial ability to purchase before bringing them to and through a home, and especially in negotiating the sale price and helping with the financing. Show the sellers examples of the type of advertising your agency most frequently uses, and give them an approximation of how often advertisements on their home will appear. (Whenever these ads do appear, clip them out and mail them to those sellers, even if you are 100 percent sure that they will read them in their local paper. Everyone likes to know he is being remembered. And remembering helps you get extensions, renewals, and referrals.)

DISCUSS EXPIRATION DATE

Everyone would like to take listings for as long a term as possible; it's guaranteed money. But many sellers are wary of commiting themselves to six months or longer in this volatile real estate market. So ask for less. Say to your sellers something like: "Right now most houses in this area are taking nearly four months to sell. Of course, yours may go much sooner, or if we're very unlucky, it could even take a little longer. We'd like to take your listing for just ninety days. This length of time will give you a chance to see the kind of service we provide, and will give us a chance to get your house sold. If not, at the end of ninety days you may sign an extension of the listing contract with us, or you are free to change to another agency or to try to sell the house yourself. What do you think? Isn't it worth a try?"

DISCUSS COMMISSION

Years ago Real Estate Boards set down the "approved" or "standard" commission, and everyone signed listings at that commission rate. It is a different ball game today. There are *no* approved or standard rates. Every commission agreement is negotiable between Seller and Agent. You must tell this to your prospective clients, but you should also explain to them that offering an especially low commission rate is likely to diminish the number of showings on their home. Few agents will drive out of their way for a 4 percent commission, when they can show houses in the same price range at a 6 percent commission. Signing at the generally prevailing rate in the area is probably best. Signing at a slightly higher rate may bring a little more activity, but will not necessarily sell the property more quickly.

Also with the end of standard commission came the development of what I call "creative commission." Some agencies are now offering sliding-scale commissions such as: 6 percent of the first $100,000, 4 percent of the next $75,000, and 3 percent of anything above that. Or another variation: 5 percent of the first $50,000, and 7 percent of anything above that. Or almost any other combination.

If your company uses these innovations, you must explain them carefully to your prospective sellers so that they understand what they are signing in the listing contract. A good way to do the explanation is to work all the figures out on paper at an ideal price. For example: "At a selling price of $87,000, Mr. & Mrs. Homeowner, you will be required to pay commission as follows . . ."

In some states, laws are now being formulated and put into effect that will require real estate agents to give both buyers and sellers an estimate of closing costs either upon signing the listing agreement or before signing the sales contract. Check with your broker or your local real estate board to find out the status of cost disclosure legislation in your area.

ASK FOR THE LISTING

This is the step that puts fear into the hearts of many new agents. They are excellent up to the point of saying, "May we take your listing?" but those words seem to stick in their throats. These agents feel awkward about asking for signatures, about asking sellers to make a commitment. Yet the direct question is the best way of getting the listing. Even if your sellers say, "We'd like to think about it," they owe you an answer and you therefore have the opportunity to call them back.

"Ask and you shall receive" is a message for all aspects of human life.

EIGHT

Customers

"GOOD morning, ABC Realty. Ann Seller speaking."

"Hello. I'm calling about the ranch you advertised in the paper last night. The one with the swimming pool."

"Yes, that's a beautiful house. What can I tell you about it?"

"I'd like to know where it is."

"That house is on Pine View Road."

"Oh, OK. Thanks. We really don't want that section of town." *Click.*

This kind of phone conversation is a leading cause of migraines among brokers, whether they realize it or not. Every real estate broker advertises his listings and hopes that the ads will bring in customers for those listings. In reality, however, he knows that this rarely happens. Only a small number of customers (somewhere in the range of 3 percent) actually buy the advertised house that prompted their call. It is an axiom in the business, therefore, that a call in response to a newspaper ad is a call from a customer in search of an agent. When that customer fails to make real contact with the agent who answers his/her call, the broker loses advertising money and both the broker and the sales agent lose potential commission money.

In short, Ann Seller fumbled the call for the house on Pine View Road. She missed the cue in the caller's opening remarks that he was really interested in the swimming pool, and she never even got his name. At no time during the conversation did she respond as a trained sales agent. Instead she cordially answered the caller's question while making no effort to direct the conversation. Unfortunately this kind of telephone technique is extremely common among beginning agents (and even among some of the experienced ones). All of which is exactly the reason some larger firms will not allow new agents to answer the phone until several months after they begin work.

Let's look at what Ann Seller might have done with that call.

"Good morning, ABC Realty. Ann Seller speaking."

"Hello. I'm calling about the ranch you advertised in the paper last night. The one with the swimming pool."

"Yes. That's a beautiful house and the pool is really extraordinary. It's an in-ground unit that uses a heavy vinyl liner. This particular one is painted with beautiful plants, coral, and tropical fish. Have you ever seen this type of pool?"

Here Ann has picked up on the interest in the pool. She gives some specific and enticing information and then takes control of the conversation by asking a question.

The caller responds, "No, I haven't personally, but I've heard they're pretty good. How big is it? I have a son on the swim team."

Pride prompted the last sentence and it tells Ann a lot. This is a family man calling and at least one of his children is old enough to be on a swim team. The odds are that these are not first home buyers.

"The pool is forty feet long, Mr.——. Oh, I'm sorry, I didn't get your name."

"O'Brian. John O'Brian."

Now Ann has taken the first step to acquiring a new customer, getting his/her name. She needn't worry about the address, that can come later. Meanwhile she can use the customer's name during the conversation to establish better rapport.

"Yes, Mr. O'Brian. I think your son could do laps pretty well in that length. There's also a diving board and a wading area. Do you have other children?"

Ann is again controlling the conversation with questions and acquiring more information.

"Yeah, two others, younger. We're really looking for a bigger house."

"Well this particular house has only three bedrooms but they are large, and it has an absolutely wonderful family room with French doors opening on the patio/pool area and a tremendous, sunny, eat-in kitchen."

"Hey, that sounds great! My wife and I love to cook. It'd be nice to have a kitchen big enough so we won't bump into each other all the time!" He laughs. Mr. O'Brian is warming to Ann Seller and to her description of the property. He no longer feels defensive and uncomfortable in his phone conversation. He continues, "Can you tell me where this house is? We'd like to drive by."

"Certainly, Mr. O'Brian. The house is on Pine View Road. Do you know the area?" Again Ann is keeping control with another question.

"Oh yeah, that's a pretty busy street and hilly. I couldn't let my little ones ride their bikes there at all. I don't think we'd be interested in that house after all."

"Oh, I'm sorry to hear that. Large pools are hard to find. But I do know of another house with an all-ceramic pool in Martinsville. Would you be interested in looking at that? It's only about twenty minutes from Bedford."

"No, I don't think so. The schools there aren't as good as the ones we have here."

"Yes, I agree, schools are really important. I'll tell you what, Mr. O'Brian, I have some free time this afternoon and if you're interested, I'll go through my listings book to see what I can find with a pool and good schools and a big kitchen. Then I can make copies of the listings and send them to you to look at at home."

"You know that's a really good idea. I'd really appreciate that."

Mr. O'Brian now feels indebted to Ann Seller. She has offered him a service which makes his house hunting easier. He is not feeling pressured since she has not asked him to come down to the office or tried to make an appointment to show him houses.

Ann continues. "OK, that's great. Just let me take your address and I'll get whatever I can find into the mail for you tonight."

"John O'Brian, 44 Winding Road, Brookfield."

"And your phone number just in case I stumble on something stupendous that I can't wait to tell you about."

"Do you think you will?"

"No, but you never can tell. New things are always coming out on the flash sheet."

"OK. It's 555-6432."

"555-6432, good. Oh, and just one more thing, Mr. O'Brian. How about the price range? Do you have a top dollar figure in mind?"

"Well, we figure we can probably go to 120 tops; if we get 95 for this house, that is."

"Oh, I see. Do you have your present house listed for sale now?"

"No, but Martha and I figure it's gotta be worth 95, especially since that new office building moved in and things started really selling again."

"It may be, Mr. O'Brian, or it may be worth even more. There's a really accurate way to find out. It's called a competitive market analysis and we offer it free. I'll send you some information about it with the listings, OK?"

Ann now sees potential for a double deal, both listing and sale. Her approach however is low key. She introduces the idea of getting an accurate evaluation of the worth of the O'Brian's present house, but does not force the issue of trying to make contact. She has all the information she needs from John O'Brian at this point. After sending her mailing, she will get in touch with him again.

Mr. O'Brian is not only unthreatened, but actually interested. He responds, "Yeah, that sounds good. We'll be watching for your envelope."

Ann can mail the O'Brians the information she promised, or if their house is not far out of her way, she can hand deliver it on her way home. This gives her an opportunity to actually see their property. She should introduce herself and simply leave the envelope with the person who opens the door. It would be a serious mistake to enter the property uninvited at this point. Sellers want their homes to look their best when shown, and that means to agents as well as to buyers. Ann should therefore call back a day or two later and ask the O'Brians what they thought of the material she left. At this point, she should try to make an appointment for a competitive market analysis, stressing that there is no obligation whatsoever.

If the O'Brians are serious buyers, she will be invited in. She should bring comparables and do a thorough and accurate market analysis. Then she should discuss financing a larger home with the O'Brians, pointing out to them a realistic top dollar figure. And always she should listen to their hopes and motivations in making this move. After this kind of thoroughly professional introduction, making appointments to inspect houses for sale will be but the natural growth of a well-tended seed.

You're probably thinking that this is a nice little scenario, but that the real world doesn't always work out this way. And you're right. Every phone call is a little different; each presents slightly different problems and stumbling blocks, and some are simply duds—nothing could make them work right for you. But there are a few universals—or "almost" universals—and knowing them will vastly improve your phone technique. Be aware that every potential buyer who calls your office has been interested by something in the ad he or she read. Try to discover the motivation for calling. Be aware that the goal of an agent answering the phone is not selling a house by phone, but meeting the caller. Know that good phone technique is always the same: control of the conversation, specific information, and cordiality. And most important of all, know that the finest working tool you have as a real estate agent is the valuable service you offer without high-powered sales pressure. That service might be an offer to show the callers the house they phoned about; or to send them information on some other houses currently available; or to do a competitive market analysis on the house they now own; or to provide them with printed material on current interest rates and mortgage qualification guidelines at area lending institutions.

This last item—financing information—is especially effective in dealing with first home buyers. Explain to them in the course of your phone conversation that you have all this information on file in your office along with tables of tax rates for every town in the area. Suggest to them that they spend twenty minutes finding out exactly how much house they can afford before spending hours house hunting in a price range either too high or too low. And offer to provide them with tax tables for your area. (You can also provide street maps if your broker has them available for free distribution.) Few serious buyers will hesitate to come down to your office once they are offered this kind of valuable information without a hard sell. And once they come to the office and meet you, you are on your way to a sale. Your success then depends on your ability, your personality, your perceptiveness, your efficiency, and sometimes on a little bit of luck.

The efficiency starts with a careful qualification of your buyers. To find the right house for any customers, you need to know what he or she or they can afford to pay. On paper that may sound simple, but qualifying buyers is the biggest stumbling block most agents encounter, with the possible exception of negotiating. And negotiating itself would most often be easier if the buyers had been properly qualified.

So what's the problem? Why do even experienced agents stumble over qualification? It's money. Most people find it difficult to ask another person or couple how much they make, how much they have managed to save, how much they owe, and how much they are willing to stretch for a house. Yet the answers to all these questions are essential to effective work in real estate sales. Without this information, you as an agent can waste hours of your time and a good deal of gas in your car showing houses your customers cannot possibly afford. And/or you can spend hours negotiating a deal that cannot be made or that will fall through at the bank. And what will you get for your effort? You will lose the confidence and trust of both your clients (the seller) and your customers (the buyers). It will be *no sale, final.*

In a sentence then: *You must qualify all your customers.* The only question is "How?"

Some agents conduct rather formal qualification interviews, asking their questions from behind a desk and writing the information they obtain in a notebook. The reaction of most buyers to this method is defensive. They feel interrogated and intimidated and often provide rather sketchy information. Other agents err in the opposite direction. They sprinkle their qualification questions into the conversation as they show the day's tour of houses. This method is inaccurate and unreliable at best. The qualification method of choice, in my opinion, is the printed mortgage application form coupled with absolute openness of purpose on the part of the agent.

Here's how to work with it. Once you have met a home-buying couple and established some rapport, simply explain that in order to do your job most efficiently and effectively—that is, in order to find them the best house that they can afford—you must work with accurate financial facts. Assure them, "These are the same financial statistics that a lending institution will require when you apply for a mortgage. In fact, this is a copy of a mortgage application form from Home and Hearth Savings Bank." (Or use your own agency printed form headed "Mortgage Qualification Information" and say "This form is patterned after the mortgage application forms of several leading area lenders.")

Provide your customers with pencils, a place to write, and unpressured time, and then leave them to their work, explaining, "When you have this filled out, we'll go over it together and then you'll know just where you stand in terms of bank qualification. Then you can stop worrying about money and concentrate on getting a good house."

I don't mean these last quotations as a canned speech to be memorized (that never works), but as a sample of a working approach to qualification. It is an approach that reassures the customers that the financial information you are requesting is necessary because it is exactly the information that will be requested in order to obtain a mortgage and therefore to buy a house. Most buyers are actually relieved to put the information down on paper and to discuss it with someone in the field before they need to approach a bank.

Occasionally, however, you will come across buyers who balk at the idea of discussing their financial position with an agent, or you will be working with friends and find the qualifying process awkward and embarrassing. In these special cases, the minimum amount of information that you need as an agent is the intended amount of your buyer's down payment and the amount of mortgage they expect to carry. (The two add up to the cost of the house.) To save yourself from difficulties, however, suggest strongly that these buyers meet privately with a loan officer of their bank and discuss that bank's qualification and loan policies. And give them some printed information on mortgage qualification guidelines at several other institutions. After their interview and study of the guidelines, ask them directly if their calculations corresponded with their banker's, or if they have made any adjustments in their house-hunting price range. This is not the best of all possible methods, but at least it puts your buyers in touch with some realistic numbers and limits to some degree your potential headaches.

There is more to selling residential real estate than financial and investment statistics, however, How much a couple can afford is one part of the picture (the rational side), what they want is the other part (the emotional side). Now we get into home and all the connotations of the word. We also get into the world of feelings where the real estate agent is often asked to perform as part-time psychologist, psychic, magician, counselor, and friend.

It's a hard act to master and a harder one to keep on stage. So hard in fact that I suggest you duck it and hand the emotional responsibilities back to your customers. Do this by asking them to draw up a "Need and Want" list—two columns, one for what they absolutely *must* have in a house, and the other for what they *want,* in the order of importance. Keep a copy of their list in your working file. Add items, move them from one column to the other or up or down in a column, or delete them as ideas change in the course of the house hunting. And then use the list as a rational lifeline in the stormy sea of negotiating.

The "Need and Want" list is rarely compiled while your customers are at your office. It just takes too much time and too much talking over. It is usually done at home (or in a motel at night in the case of transferees) and then brought along on the next scheduled day of house hunting. When you first see this list, read through it carefully and discuss each item and its motivating factors with your customers. What is written doesn't always mean what it seems to, so don't jump to any conclusions. For example, when one couple writes "full dry basement" at the top of their want list, they mean storage space; another couple is thinking about a workshop; another a dark room; another a place to do oil paintings on the weekends; another a place to build a playroom for the children; another a place to keep the dogs during the work day; another nothing more than good resale value.

Talk with your customers and listen to what they say very carefully. Knowledge of the character and makeup of a home-buying family, its hobbies and interests, its plans and goals, is essential to your professional work as an agent. The more you know about your people, the faster you will find the right house for them, and the more confidence they will have in your work.

But despite all the diversity among people and this very real need to know your customers individually, buyers *can* be separated into two very broad categories: local buyers and out-of-area buyers. Everybody is one or the other and your working method will be determined by which.

OUT-OF-AREA BUYERS

You should consider anyone moving more than fifteen miles an out-of-area buyer. Even though a particular couple may have shopped or worked or driven through the town or towns you work in for ten years, they cannot and will not know the area as intimately as a person who has lived there. Part of your role as an agent for out-of-area customers therefore will be something between tour guide and teacher.

These two roles increase in importance when you are working with corporate transferees from other states, with the added dimension and problem of time pressure. Many transferees have one week to tour an area and select a home. They usually are extremely loyal customers, however, because they do not have the time to agent shop or swap. And vice versa, most agents are extremely loyal agents, clearing all nonessentials from their schedules and devoting the week entirely to that transferee customer.

It may surprise you, however, to learn that really top agents spend a great deal of time in their offices when working with out-of-area buyers. And the degree of their success (and the number of referrals that come later) often depends upon how well they've done their homework.

"What homework?" you ask.

"The *unassigned* homework," is your answer. The same kind of work that makes for honor graduates and million-dollar sales club real estate agents. The work that no one *has* to do, but, when done, lifts an agent head and shoulders above her colleagues.

Let me outline a general plan for you to use with out-of-area buyers. You may change it, or add to it, or delete parts of it according to your personal style and the needs of your community, but it will give you some direction.

1. Draw up a sheet which you can type and copy or have printed similar to the following:

WHY LOCATION?

What are the most important things to look for when buying a home? There is a real estate adage that answers, "Location! Location! and Location!" The adage is true. There is nothing that will affect the value of your home investment more than its location. And "Location! Location! and Location!" translates into town, neighborhood, and lot.

TOWN

Judge taxes, services, schools, and judge its character and personality.

NEIGHBORHOOD

Is it homogeneous or heterogenous? Is it well maintained, being revitalized, or slipping? Where does "our" house fit in the neighborhood's price range?

LOT

Is it attractive? Accessible? Protected from commercial encroachment?

2. Draw up another sheet or sheets or booklet titled:

TAXES AND WHAT YOU GET FOR YOUR MONEY

Here list each of the towns in which you work, its tax rate, its assessment policy, and its services. For example:

Johnson City. Tax rate 5.49 mills on 100 percent assessment. Last tax reassessment 1978. Next reassessment scheduled 1983. Sewers in some areas; sewer use fee $90 a year. City water throughout supplied by Valley Water Company, an independent commercial company. Police force: 86 full-time men and women, 33 part-time crossing guards and auxiliaries. Fire department: 7 full-time men and a large professionally trained volunteer force. Government: elected mayor (full time) and city council. Library: one, open six days a week. Recreation: seven parks with tennis courts, baseball fields, and a year-round recreation program. One outdoor municipal pool: fee $80 per year per family.

3. Draw up individual sheets or a booklet titled:

MEET OUR COMMUNITIES

Generally each page or entry here will deal with a separate municipality, but if you work in a very large city, you may wish to discuss individual neighborhoods or areas.

The purpose of these profiles is to try to capture a sense of the character of an area so that newcomers can get an idea of how their family life-style would fit in. Be honest and unprejudiced in your profile and don't ignore racial and ethnic sub-communities; they are a part of our life in this country and to omit them from a profile is a mark of prejudice and a disservice to your customers. Here's another fictitious example of how this information might be organized.

Heightstown. Population 60,000; a suburban community with a commercial center and one shopping mall, some light industry, research facilities, and several office buildings. The median house sale price in 1980 was $89,000, more than $20,000 above the national median. The range of house sale prices was from $37,000 to $287,000. This is generally a middle to upper middle class community. There are some areas of apartments and least-cost housing, however, and some exclusive three- and five-acre estates. The town has a blend of white, black, Hispanic, and foreign citizens. There is an active Jewish community and an Oriental neighborhood which features the finest Chinese restaurant in our state. There are three Catholic churches, eight Protestant churches, two Jewish synagogues, and a number of smaller religious communities. There are a drama group, an art league, a community concert series, a model railroad club, stamp, coin, and bridge groups, Boy Scouts and Girl Scouts, 4-H, an active newcomers group, and an excellent library.

4. Draw up a sheet or sheets or a booklet titled:

THE SCHOOLS

Schools are among the top five factors considered by transferees when choosing a community and your information should be a good deal more specific than "Oh, yes, we have good schools." For each town you serve list how the physical plant facilities are utilized (K thru 6, 7 thru 9, and a 3-year high school, or K thru 4, 5 thru 8, and a 4-year high school, or whatever the particular plan). Get information from the board of education in each town telling about groupings in the lower grades, special educational programs for handicapped, slower, or gifted students, art and music programs, athletics, and college and vocational training. And obtain and file in your office a supply of whatever pamphlets and booklets the school board in each town has available.

Compiling these four informational guides is no easy job, I know. I'm asking you to put in a good deal of time which seems to have no immediate financial reward. But the reward will come, I assure you, and once you do this job, it's done. It can be easily maintained by simply updating on an annual basis, perhaps during the slow season of November and December, or the dog days of August. Also you don't have to do this work alone. Most brokers are delighted to help and will often pay the costs of printing, and the agents in many offices put the material together as a group.

If your office does have a group project, however, don't forget to personalize the information you give to *your* customers. Make copies of single sheets for yourself by taping your card in the corner of the master sheet before you use the copy machine. Or if you have printed booklets, staple your card to every booklet you distribute. You want your customers to have your name and phone number available whenever they have a question on the material you have given them.

With all of your homework done and filed neatly in a desk drawer or the office supply cabinet, you should still begin each interview with out-of-area buyers with a qualification sheet. Once you determine the price range of their house hunting, you can go to a large (wall-size) street map, point out and discuss the various towns or areas that you work in, and show your customers where they will be most likely to find a house in their price range. Some very large firms have even gone so far as to make movies of the various towns they serve. These are also used as an introductory tool.

Now give your customers the four information profiles you have prepared, street maps, and any other municipal information you have in the office. The League of Women Voters, historical societies, recreation departments, some banks, local libraries, special interest groups, and many large corporations print flyers and brochures about their towns. Gather as many as you can and keep them on file in the office. This material may seem dull and trivial to you, but it is fascinating reading at night in a motel room when you are trying to decide where you will live for the next three to five years or more.

After talking with your customers about their housing needs and goals and telling them about the communities you work in, choose three or four houses from your listing book that they find interesting and make appointments to inspect them. Three or four is not too few. That first day out you are introducing your customers to the communities you serve. There will be much driving and little stopping. Show them the shopping centers, the churches, the schools, the parks, the theaters, the restaurants. Remember they are town and neighborhood hunting as well as house hunting. Near the end of the day, talk with them about which towns or areas seem most appealing to them and then make an appointment for another day during which you will concentrate on showing houses in those areas.

When working with transferees, be particularly careful not to over-schedule a day. It's a good idea to choose ten or twelve listings in one town or area before your customers arrive and then discuss these listings with them. Let them weed out those they do not want, but feel free to make comments on the special features which prompted you to choose a particular listing. They may change their minds after listening to you. Then schedule your showings in a circle if you can so that you do not waste a great deal of time crisscrossing your own tracks. And don't hesitate to stop for coffee, lunch, or whatever breaks seem appropriate during the day. House hunting is very tiring and pauses can refresh and revitalize, and sometimes promote an enthusiastic response to the next house in line.

LOCAL BUYERS

Working with local buyers is another ball game. You can give them copies of all the written material you prepared for your out-of-area customers; you can discuss zoning policies, taxes, schools, and neighborhoods with them; you can carefully pinpoint street locations and trace your proposed house-hunting routes on a wall map for them, and they will probably think you efficient and industrious. But these services, so important and impressive to the stranger in town, will rarely help you sell a house to a local resident.

When people choose to move within the same town, they usually have very well-crystallized ideas about why they are moving and what they want in their new house. Usually it is a larger, better, or newer house and/or a better or more convenient neighborhood. Almost nothing of what you say will influence their opinions or goals. They are already experts on the town, or so they believe. You'll hear things like, "We know this place, we've been here seven years now, you know, and we want to live in the Brookside area. Everyone knows it's the best."

"Everyone knows" in that sentence means "we believe" and that "we believe" can be as emotionally rooted as it can be rational. Perhaps a relative or good friend lives in Brookside, or perhaps the husband's boss just bought a house there, or perhaps PTA small talk has it that the Brookside Elementary School is far superior to the other schools in town. It doesn't matter. Usually you'll never find out all of the many reasons behind the choices.

The point is that success with local buyers demands a different type of skill and efficiency. And it demands intuition. Listen to and watch your local customers. What are the various motives that you hear when they talk about their desire for a new house? What does their "Need and Want" list reveal? What do they appreciate and comment about in the houses that you show them? What do they disregard? When you put the pieces of this puzzle together, the picture of the house you get may be different from the type you thought you were looking for. Think, and listen with an inner ear and look with a third eye.

Let me give you some examples. You have a young family who says they want a two-story colonial and *only* a colonial, yet you know the couple plans to have more children and you see the woman straining as she carries her tired two-year-old on her hip up the stairs. You know of a ranch-style home in their price range that has a family room adjacent to the kitchen. It also has a gracious "colonial" decor throughout. Wouldn't you ask them to take a look at it?

Or how about the family that wants the Brookside area and *only* the Brookside area? You know of a new development about to get under way where the houses will be in the same price range as Brookside, where the children will attend the same school, and where the land is a little higher and better drained. Wouldn't you suggest a walking tour of the land and an appointment with the builder?

Working with local buyers is often more difficult than working with out-of-area customers. They are rarely under time pressure to buy because most of them want to find their new home before they sell the one in which they are living. Most are also looking for a home rather than a house or a good investment, and they allow their emotions free rein in influencing their choice. Most local buyers will read the houses for sale section of their local papers every night, and most will run down the for-sale-by-owner ads that sound appealing. Many will also work with several different real estate firms in the same area despite the fact that you explain carefully that you can provide all the information on and show any house listed on the local Multiple Listing Service.

In other words the game played with local buyers is less rational and more competitive, and your chances of winning, of making a good sale, are less secure. But still there are skills and methods that will increase the odds in your favor.

Besides your intuition and careful observation of motivations and preferences, the most important of these skills and methods is your effective use of the Multiple Listing Service. When you work with local buyers, you must keep abreast of each and every new listing in the town where they want to live. If a good house for your customers comes through and you don't see it or don't call them on it that day, someone else will. And often it's a drop-everything-and-find-the-time-to-show-it situation.

All of this means that after the first meeting or two with local home buyers, you will rarely schedule tours that take in several houses in one day. You will much more often show individual houses, and often you will show the house to the wife alone during the daytime working hours and then, if she likes it, to the couple together in the evening or on the weekend.

You will also often meet your customers at the property to be shown rather than at your office. Avoid, however, giving out the address on a new listing and suggesting that your customers drive by. "Drive-bys" are most often the death of a sale. Houses sell because people see them inside and out. Also, the only way you can be assured of getting your share of the commission on the sale of a house is to be instrumental in that sale. In most cases that means walking on the property with your potential buyers.

There is one other service that you as an agent can provide for both local and out-of-area buyers and which is especially influential in determining the success of your career. You've probably already guessed it: help with mortgaging. Here you must take on the role of teacher, for most families, even the best educated, know little about the intricacies of the mortgage market. To take on the role of teacher, however, you must first become a student. Read all the information you can find on the various kinds of mortgages and then gather data on the exact amounts of application fees, appraisal fees, points, mortgage origination fees, legal review fees, mortgage insurance fees, and all the other costs involved in getting a mortgage at each of the major lending institutions in your area. Keep records and keep your records accurate.

Then, when you can find an hour to spare, but definitely before you begin negotiations on a particular house, sit down with your customers and explain the differences between, and the advantages and disadvantages of, conventional mortgages and FHA and VA mortgages, and privately insured mortgages, and wrap-around mortgages, and roll-over mortgages, and variable interest rate mortgages, and balloon mortgages, and assumptions with or without secondary financing.

Discuss the interest rates and down payment requirements at the various lending institutions. And point out to your buyers that heavy application fees, appraisal fees, mortgage origination fees, points, or required insurance at a particular lender can more than wipe out the apparent advantage of a ¼ percent lower interest rate.

Lending mortgage money is a competitive business just like any other competitive business in this country, and you as an agent can do much to teach your home buyers how to shop for the best deal. The information you give them will be information that they take with them through every house-hunting experience of their lives and it will invariably save them many thousands of dollars. It will also assure you of their loyalty and their referrals.

NINE

Negotiating

WHILE in college I took a course in American Government, only because a course in American Government was required for teacher certification. I fully expected to be bored by a tedious survey of constitutional law and bureaucratic structure. But the semester began with Allen Drury's *Advise and Consent,* and I was *not* bored. That book and that course were my first real introduction to government and to the meaning of negotiation.

I discovered that the Congress of the United States functions within the formal structure of the American Constitution, but that the real work of the men and women who make up that Congress is only tangentially related to law in the abstract. Their real responsibility is the job of getting things done in a huge and complicated society. It requires knowledge, drive, assertiveness, flexibility, manipulation, and most of all negotiation—the art of knowing how to give a little to get a little.

And everything I just said about the work of the members of Congress can be said on a different plane about the work of real estate agents. To get a real estate license, an agent must study and know the real estate laws of her state, and she must learn how to work effectively within those laws.

Like the novice member of Congress, however, though she may know real estate law extremely well, she will still have to learn much about how to get things done in her profession through her own observation, trial, and error. This knowledge from experience is nowhere more important and nowhere more difficult to come by than in the art of negotiation.

I will try to share with you some "how-to" information that I've learned by doing, but first we must review what is required by law.

THE LAW OF AGENCY

To discuss real estate law state by state would require volumes (indeed there are volumes already published on it), but a basic legal attitude regarding the agency relationship prevails across the country. The concept of agency relationship sets out the boundaries which you must recognize before you can begin to work and negotiate effectively. Some of the material in the next few paragraphs may bring back memories of your pre-license courses, so I will try to be as brief as possible.

When homeowners sign a listing contract, they essentially hire a broker to act as their agent, promising to pay him/her a commission for procuring a ready, willing, and able buyer at a price and terms acceptable to the sellers. Throughout the country laws state that in performing the role of agent for the sellers, the broker is required to make a continuous, bona fide effort to find a buyer for the property and to maintain a fiduciary (trust) relationship with his client (the sellers). Courts virtually everywhere have been firm in finding for the necessity and importance of the trust relationship. It is the broker's duty to represent the property honestly, but also to respect the financial and personal confidences that are entrusted to him.

Misrepresentation or failure to disclose factual information pertinent to the sale or market value of the property to the buyers is also a breach of the agency relationship. In most states, any action that is unprofessional, dishonest, underhanded, or in any way incongruent with the agency relationship established in the listing contract can be subject to legal action, which just about everywhere includes the possibility of the loss of your license.

In order to protect sellers against the purchase of their properties for investment and quick profit based upon "inside" information, every broker and all salespersons in his/her employ must also disclose any personal interest in the transfer of real property. That is, he/she must inform the seller if he/she or any member of their immediate family is a member of the purchasing party.

You've probably noticed that I've been talking about the responsibilities of the broker thus far through this section, and you're probably thinking "I'm only a sales agent, not a broker, what are *my* responsibilities?"

As I explained in Chapter 3, essentially the responsibilities of a sales agent in the agency relationship are the same as those of the broker for whom she works. An agency relationship can only be established with a real estate *broker.* (This is why the broker and not the sales agent must sign the listing contract.) However, the sales agent is required to work under the supervision of her broker and is bound to conduct business in accord with the broker's policies, standards, and legal requirements.

Essentially then an agency relationship requires the broker and his sales agents to work in the best interests of the sellers while bound also by the doctrine of elementary fair conduct. In handling the sale of real property, however, there are certain things a broker or sales agent may *not* do. He or she may not act in the role of an attorney. Most states do allow brokers and sales agents to fill in the blanks on printed real estate contracts, but they do not allow them to make any significant changes in those contracts, such as establishing a life estate or restricting certain uses of the property. State laws also do not allow brokers or sales agents to give advice on the validity of any real estate titles, and they do not allow them to advise buyers or sellers on their legal rights in a transaction. These functions are reserved to lawyers.

Purchasing and owning real property can have many legal entanglements. Of course many deals can seem eminently simple when buyers and sellers are in complete agreement and both riding a wave of enthusiasm. Everyone, including you, the agent, wants the agreement in writing, and it is very easy for the agent to fill in the blanks on the contract and then witness the signatures. In fact, it is probably the way the majority of real estate contracts are still made in this country.

It is here, however, that I must take a stand that is often unpopular among brokers and other agents. I firmly believe that both buyers and sellers should have the contract to purchase reviewed by their own attorney before signing. Why? Because *every* real estate transaction has within it the potential of becoming both complex and controversial. I feel that many problems (and severe headaches) can be averted or diminished if legal advice is sought before entering into the contract. And, if problems should arise after the signing of contracts, both buyers and sellers have then established contact with a professional who is qualified to assist them, yet who does not have a financial stake in the completion of the deal.

In some states lawyers routinely supervise the entire closing procedure; in others title companies, banks, or other closing specialists handle the transaction. Where the lawyers routinely close, review of the contract before signing usually will not cost either party any additional fee. In areas where lawyers are not present at the closing, reviewing or drawing up a contract will involve a fee; however, it is usually not large. I strongly recommend that you as an agent at least inform your buyers and sellers that the option of professional contract review is available to them. It may slow things by a day or two, but it can make the road much smoother in the weeks that follow.

If buyers (or you as an agent) are worried that someone else might come along and offer a higher price while the contracts are being drawn or sellers are worried that the buyers might find something else cheaper or that they like better, you can somewhat protect all parties by drawing up a binder, accepting an earnest money deposit, and reporting the house "on deposit" to the MLS.

Just about every office has some kind of printed binder form somewhere in the supply closet. Find it, and check it out. It should include the date, the name and address of the buyers, the name of the sellers, and the address of the property being sold, and the amount of the purchase price. It *must* also include a statement to the effect that *"This agreement is subject to contracts being drawn by a reputable attorney which are satisfactory to both parties."* Without that statement, your little binder can become a legal contract with monstrous potential problems. There should also be included on the binder a cut-off date for the drawing or review of the contracts. Three business days is sufficient.

If the deal falls through—that is if those contracts never do get drawn and signed—you will have to return the earnest money to the buyers, and report the property back on the market to the MLS.

Just to summarize, you know now that in all the business of the real estate game, and especially in negotiating, you must be diligent, honest, loyal to your clients, and careful not to misrepresent or fail to disclose any pertinent information. That is the law. Now the question is how do you work within the law to get two parties to come to an agreement on price and terms?

This is where art comes into the business. No two deals are exactly alike, therefore no two negotiations are exactly alike, and therefore every negotiation requires judgment, skill, and art. I can set down for you some tried and tested guidelines, some "usually happens"; you will have to judge whether and when to use which. You may stumble at first. Everyone in this field feels she has lost some deals that she should have been able to put together. But be aware of what you are doing, of the steps you are taking. Try to watch yourself by standing back from your feelings after the negotiating is over and judging what you did by rational standards of good business practice. You might even talk over the process occasionally with your office manager or broker. If you do this, you will improve in competence and effectiveness with each deal you make.

GETTING THE FIRST OFFER

Buying a house is a scary thing for most people. It's a big bucks investment for everyone, and many people have a difficult time making the decision to make an offer. Some agents try to precipitate action with time pressure or scare tactics. How many times has the sentence, "Well, there are several other buyers interested and it might be gone tomorrow" been used? The line is as limp and fragile as a five-year-old dollar bill. And though it may heighten the anxiety of the buyers, it rarely stimulates them to make an offer they would not have made in any case.

Ineptly applied and unnecessary time pressure in real estate usually causes problems rather than progress toward a deal. It is probably the largest single cause of back outs, second thoughts, cold feet, and stop payment orders on earnest money checks.

As a responsible agent, your goal is to get a sincere first offer, and there are ways to move your buyers in that direction without the hurry-ups. In the first place, it is essential that your buyers really like the house. Usually there is little doubt in the mind of an agent when a couple is seriously interested in a property. The inspection takes longer, rooms are revisited and revisited again, the cellar, the lot boundaries, and the condition of the roof become important, and questions come up about taxes, heating costs, and schools. And then of course there is the voicing of the strongest clue to buying readiness, the single objection. It always begins, "Oh, I wish this house didn't have" and then the possibilities are limitless: a green kitchen floor, pink tile in the bath room, blue carpeting, a leaky roof, a steep driveway, a corner lot, etc.

The buyer is really saying, "I want this house, but I don't like this particular aspect of it," and this is a much stronger peg upon which to hang a sale than time pressure. Your selling tool is the question, "Would you buy it if" . . . it had a new kitchen floor, the bathroom were blue, the carpet didn't stay with the house, the roof were repaired, the driveway were level, etc. You are looking for, no, expecting an answer of yes. When you get it, you have a potential sale. You need only handle the objection.

The satisfaction of some objections like a new kitchen floor, or tearing up the carpet and sanding and refinishing the floors, or repairing the roof, can be negotiated with the price and stipulated in a contract. Encourage your buyers to make their offer with the contingency that their objections are remedied.

Other objections such as a steep driveway or an exposed corner lot cannot be changed. Your selling method then is: "Every house has flaws; there really is no perfect property anywhere. The real questions are, do you like this house and how much is it worth to you to put up with this particular flaw? Perhaps we can work out a price that will make the driveway seem more level!" Smile.

The "Need and Want" list that your buyers gave you during their initial interview and qualification becomes another invaluable tool in assisting them toward the decision to buy. Get it out and measure the house they are now considering point by point against the list. If your buyers are at all hesitant, make a copy of the list and suggest that they take it home and test it on the house again after doing the memory drawings of the floor plan and imagining a day living there. Then suggest that they plan to revisit the property the following day for a more rational and thorough inspection.

Having done the floor-plan exercise and a good deal of talking to each other, and having slept on it, your buyers will be more self-assured (and probably more critical) on their second visit to the house, but if they agree to make that return visit, you can be sure they are very serious about the property. Try to arrange for the sellers to be out of the house during that second visit. Give the buyers plenty of time to check out all the working systems and to imagine their future furniture arrangements. And then ask the closing questions, "Do you want this house?" and "At what price would you like to buy it?" With those answers in hand, you can proceed to the written offer.

APPROACHING THE SELLERS

Very few sellers expect to get full asking price for the house they are selling, but the amount of negotiating room in each asking price is a highly variable unknown. A great deal depends upon the reason for selling, the time and money pressures upon the sellers, local real estate market conditions, and national and regional mortgaging availability. The more you as a selling agent can learn about these factors the better will be your negotiating position. Of course the ideal situation is to be both listing and selling agent on the same house, but this happens all too seldom. Most agents, most of the time, must work at gathering information about the sellers.

A call to the listing agent while your buyers are still in the considering stage can be very enlightening. You need make no definite commitment. Simply call her, introduce yourself and your agency, and say that you have some people interested in the Quickly house. Ask how anxious the Quicklys are to move. Do they want an early or a long closing? Has there been much activity on their house? Are there any particular marital problems, liens on the property, or financial difficulties that you should know about? And most important of all, "Have there been any previous offers on the house? How much? What response?" The vast majority of listing agents want their properties sold (a bird in the hand is worth two in the bush), and they don't really care which member office of the local MLS does the selling. They are therefore usually most willing to cooperate in giving background information to a prospective selling agent.

Some listing agencies insist, however, that they be a party to all negotiations. This can often be a help when the listing agent is sincerely cooperating in getting the house sold. But it can sometimes bring about problems, especially if, for example, the listing agency happens to have a prospective buyer of its own for the house.

If the listing agent should be uncooperative or unavailable, many selling agents call the sellers directly before an offer is made and tell them there are some buyers who seem especially interested in their home. The goal of this call, of course, is to get the seller involved in a conversation on selling and ascertain as much information as possible. The result of such pre-offer phone calls is usually a heightened sense of expectancy in the sellers, which of course paves the way for an offer.

While you are questioning the sellers, they may in turn ask

you some questions. Mostly they are prompted by curiosity but often by a concern about financing. These almost always deal with your buyers, their age, number of children, jobs, where they come from, etc. Answering questions of this kind is just fine, but avoid mentioning names and avoid above all any discussion of money or finances. That must be saved for the formal negotiations.

Sometimes when a buyer makes a very low first offer, agents call the sellers and present the figure over the phone. This is tantamount to saying, "Here's an offer that you want to refuse, right?" and leaves the agent in a very weak negotiating position. She is in essence the bearer of bad tidings and has had no opportunity to establish face-to-face contact with the sellers. Such a situation makes it easier and more likely for the sellers to say "no" to future offers.

Presenting an offer, even if it is obviously unacceptable, is best done in person and best done in the sellers' home. Especially when a first offer is low, you as an agent want the opportunity to be accepted into that home and the chance to establish rapport. Establishing your image as a competent, reliable, and honest agent at this point is more important than the dollar figure on that offer form. Negotiating with sellers who have confidence in your ability is much easier and more likely to succeed.

To some extent, there is a problem of stereotyping to be dealt with by women in the negotiating stage of almost every real estate transaction. The history of competent women in business is short, and as much as people and public statements would like to deny emotional attitudes and prejudices, they often persist, at least subconsciously, for decades beyond their supposed demise. Male sales agents must deal with a male stereotype of being aggressive, cagey, and manipulative. Female agents, especially when they enter upon negotiation, encounter the age-old female image of being incompetent with money, passive, and unmotivated by the real need to support themselves. No one wants to trust the negotiation on their largest lifetime investment to a scatterbrain who can't balance a checkbook, who says "yes, dear" automatically, and who is in the business because she is bored at home or likes to look at decorating in other people's houses.

You as a woman sales agent, however, can quickly put to rest your sellers' fears, unspoken prejudices, and uncertainties. At the risk of being repetitious, I suggest that the way to do this is to be professionally dressed, courteous and friendly, but not to engage in too much chitchat. Get down to business seriously, demonstrate your knowledge of the housing marketplace, and most important of all, have financial facts and figures readily available.

Always have a pocket calculator with you and become expert at its use. The ability to calculate the answers to financial questions quickly and accurately combined with an up-to-the-minute knowledge of the mortgaging policies of local banks will quickly dispel antifeminine prejudice.

The best place to present a first offer is at the kitchen table, at the heart of the house as it were, with coffee cup in hand. If the buyer's first offer is so low as to be insulting, the sellers probably won't throw you out until you finish your coffee, which of course gives you time to talk and thus time to convince them of your competence, sincerity, and commitment to do your very best to sell their home at a fair price. If the offer is an acceptable one, the table also provides space and surface for signing. If your sellers are more formal and confine you to the living room, choose a place in front of the coffee table so that you have at least that much space to spread out your papers and do calculations if necessary.

If the first offer you bring in is acceptable, and the offer forms or contracts are signed, you have an easy one. Earning your commission then usually hangs only upon the mortgage and inspection contingencies. If, as is much more often the case, the first offer is not acceptable to the sellers, you must continue working, and the next step is getting a counter offer.

When the first offer from the buyers is within striking range of the selling price that the sellers have in mind, they will usually counter with a figure slightly above their hoped-for sales figure. These deals can usually be brought together in one more step. The next and slightly higher buyer offer is usually accepted.

When the first offer is a low ball, the sellers sometimes refuse to make a counter offer. At this point, your main task is to keep the door open. The last thing you want is angry or insulted sellers when you leave the house. Explain that a feeler offer is a common practice in most business transactions—a knock at the door—and is no reflection on the sellers' home or decorating, but merely an opening to negotiation. When you hear, "We don't want any part of an offer like that or the people who would make it!" or "I wouldn't be caught dead making a counter offer to a ridiculous bid like that. What do they think we are, complete idiots? We know property value in this town. We're not stupid!", I have found the best reply to be, "Would you consider another offer?" pronounced quietly, slowly, and in a very professional manner. The sellers can hardly say "no" to the question since they want to sell their house and thus your chances of making the deal are still alive.

GETTING A HIGHER OFFER

Imagine a real estate game played by today's rules back at the turn of the century, before the phone was everywhere. If you were an agent negotiating a deal then, you might bid good-night to the sellers, get into your one-horse shay, drive to wherever your buyers were waiting, sit down with them, and tell them the details of what had transpired during your meeting with the sellers. Then you would proceed to discuss a second offer with them. You would be physically present, and presumably in control, leading and directing your buyers, answering their questions, calming their fears, dispelling their reservations, until they arrived at a second offer more likely to appeal to the sellers. Such lovely fantasy is rather like the Christmas cards you see with pretty nineteenth-century girls skating in fur-trimmed coats, their hands tucked into fluffy muffs.

However, today we do have the telephone. While it is certainly the real estate agent's most frequently used tool, its ring can also be the deathblow of a deal. Let's imagine a scene, 1980s style.

After working hard at negotiating and meeting adamant resistance from sellers who are old hands at the game and unwilling to reveal any but the most essential information, Sara Worker returns to her office and calls her potential buyers, who are anxiously waiting at home.

Sara: Hi John, this is Sara Worker.

John: Hi, what's happening?

Sara: Well, I talked with Mr. & Mrs. Peddler for almost an hour and a half. They really want to sell that house, and their ideas for closing coincide perfectly with yours. They are even willing . . .

John: *(interrupts)* Great, will they take our price?

Sara: Not exactly. I don't know how much negotiating they're really willing to do, perhaps a lot. But they felt your initial offer was a low ball, and they said that if you want to play that game, they'll counter with $1,000 off their asking price.

John: Are you kidding? That house isn't worth that! They're at least $5,000 over market value. We don't want their drapes or their carpet, and we're certainly not going to pay for that stuff. I think we'll just drop this whole thing. Thanks for your time. *Click.*

Like the presentation of initial offers, the reporting of a counter offer is another example of the devastating, impersonal effect of negotiating by phone. Again the real estate agent is left in an extremely weak position. Re-establishing contact with the buyers is difficult and borders upon either pleading or pushing, or both. And the agent certainly can't report to the sellers that the buyers slammed the phone down, or she can report that, but it won't take the negotiating very far! Everyone is at a standoff with pride getting in the way. When Sara Worker made that easy-to-do phone call instead of driving across town to her buyers' apartment, she lost control of the negotiation.

"So how do you keep control?" you ask. The answer goes back to the horse and buggy fantasy: *personal contact.* It is much more difficult to push a person out the door than to hang up the phone, and the increased difficulty allows for some thinking time, talking time, and listening time.

At the same time that you make an appointment to present a first offer to a seller, make an appointment to present the counter offer to the buyers. This is actually easier to do than it reads on the page. Simply say, "John, I have an appointment to present your offer to the Peddlers at 7 this evening. I'll probably be there an hour, maybe a little more. Will you and Alice be at home after 8 so that I might bring over the news?" I've never had anyone refuse. No one wants to wait too long to hear what happened. If you are working with out-of-town buyers, you can meet them at their hotel, or even better you can arrange that they wait for you in your office while you present their offer.

When negotiating has reached the stage of the second buyer offer, the goal of the agent is to get a good (enticing to the sellers) dollar figure. This is therefore the ideal time to bring out the comparables file or book. By showing your buyers the listings on comparable houses that have been sold during the past year, you can put them in touch with an accurate sense of market value and direct them toward a realistic offer. If they are smart, they will still bid on the low side of that market value figure, but you will be closing the gap significantly.

You may also need at this time to do a financial review of your buyers' qualifications to carry the necessary mortgage demanded by the higher offer. Here again a professional use of pencil, paper, and calculator to gather and present the figures and an absolutely thorough knowledge of your local mortgage market will dispel any subconscious prejudices about women and money and instill in your buyers respect and confidence in your ability to put the deal together fairly and ethically. It will also increase their sense of loyalty to you as their personal agent, in the event that this particular deal simply cannot be made.

THE SELLERS' SECOND CHANCE

At the risk of sounding like a stuck recording, I remind you again: When presenting the buyers' second offer, do not mention any numbers on the phone. When you call the sellers simply say, "Mrs. Peddler, my buyers have come up with another offer. I think you and Mr. Peddler will find it much more appealing. May I stop by to talk with you about it?" If you get a snarling, "It depends on how much it is. We told you what we wanted the last time you were here. What are your numbers?", stick to your position. Say, "The new offer does not meet your counter offer, but it is very much worth discussing. I'd like only a few minutes of your time."

It would be an extremely unusual seller who would not agree to meet with you. When you go to that appointment, take along the same comparables that you showed the buyers. Remember your goal is to get two parties to reach a mutual agreement on the value of the property. Those comps are invaluable because they are impartial. Also take along the mortgage calculations you made for your buyers. You may have to convince the sellers that the buyers can afford to buy the house, or (just as often) you may have to convince them that those buyers simply can't afford to go very much higher on their offering price.

At this point the sellers may accept the new offer. Then you have a deal. Or they may make a second counter just on the high side of market value. Then you may have a deal which needs only a little more work to close the gap. Or they may reject your facts and figures and emotionally stick to their asking price, which probably means that they are not really ready to sell and, therefore, you don't have a deal. Then you will have to work at keeping your customers loyal to you as you start the house hunting procedure again almost from scratch with disappointment thrown in as an extra burden.

FINE TUNING

When sellers and buyers are within a few thousand dollars of each other, the gap can usually be closed with give-a-little, get-a-little bargaining. Extras often no longer needed or wanted by the sellers such as carpeting, chandeliers, draperies, appliances, lawn furniture, gardening and lawn equipment, fireplace fixtures, etc. can save the buyers heavy out-of-pocket expenditures and entice them to add to their offering price dollars which can be financed over the life of the mortgage.

Closing and occupancy dates can be translated into convenience, comfort, and money to either the buyers or the sellers. What buyers want to store their furniture and live with relatives or in a motel while waiting for a closing date? What sellers want to move out before they have a place to move into? And worse yet, how many sellers can afford to carry two mortgages and a bridge note for very long when they have bought a new house before their old house was sold? An especially good and/or important closing date to either party can be worth thousands of dollars in negotiating space.

Sometimes finding better financing can enable buyers to come up a thousand or so in their offer, and their stretching will often stimulate sellers to come down a thousand or so. When buyers are stretched to their limit, who pays closing costs and points can become a serious item of negotiation. Strangely enough some sellers will give way here while standing absolutely firm on the named selling price. And, finally, if all else fails, some brokers are willing to offer to accept a small cut in commission if it will stimulate the two parties to agree to a contract.

SURVIVAL

Negotiating is the most difficult part of working in the real estate game. It is hard to teach and hard to learn, and sometimes it is hard to get through with your self-image and self-worth intact. As far as the teaching and learning go, I have tried to give you approaches rather than step-by-step procedures in this chapter because in negotiating there is no procedure that always works. As I mentioned earlier, negotiating involves individuals and every negotiating situation is therefore unique. In other words, no one can tell you exactly how to get signatures and an earnest money check for a house at 23 Oak Street on June 11, 1982. I *can* tell you, however, that there are three danger zones which you must avoid to ensure your real estate survival.

The first is anger. Whether the phone is slammed in your ear or you are called a jackass to your face, you cannot afford to respond in anger. Remember the sellers and buyers are under emotional strain, and you must remain as calm as possible. There will be time for apologies later, and both buyers and sellers are usually most generous in making them once disputes are resolved and the deal is put together.

The second danger zone is insult. No agent ever helped a sale with a line like "Well, what about the cost of having this place fumigated?" or perhaps "How many buyers do you think would be willing to tackle the mess you have here?" An agent with a sharp-edged tongue can antagonize a buyer or seller right out of a deal. What must be said, must be said in terms of dollars and sense, rationally, tactfully.

The third and probably the most tempting danger zone is emotional involvement. Sleepless nights and acid stomach over the fact that you can't find a buyer for the poor widow Brown's house, and worry over the worry of the poor widow Brown whom you've come to know and love are quick tickets out of the real estate marketplace. Remember above all else that you are doing a job to the best of your ability and that the world and the real estate business are just full of people and situations beyond your control. Offer your special service and knowledge as a real estate professional, but do not get your heart involved in negotiating.

And now a word about failure. Sometimes a deal that you are working on will be made no matter what you say or do because both parties are highly motivated and capable. Sometimes, however, the deal could not be made even with the negotiating assistance of a Henry Kissinger because one or the other of the parties was not ready, willing and/or able. For your survival in the real estate game, and for the survival of your positive sense of self, remember that you cannot manipulate, you can only negotiate.

TEN

Headaches and Hazards

CHARLES LAMB, the nineteenth-century essayist, described work as "that dry drudgery at the desk's dead wood."

"Hardly applicable to a real estate career," you say. "There's little enough time at the desk, and rarely a day that can be described as 'dry drudgery.'"

Perhaps. But take the phrase less literally. Say it aloud and listen to the hard sound of all those "d's" and I think you'll almost *feel* exactly what Lamb meant. Work, if we define it as those tasks by which we earn our livelihood, demands time and energy that each of us would prefer to spend pursuing pleasure. There is "dry drudgery" and there are headaches in every job, and sometimes I think real estate sales have more than their fair share of at least the latter.

But—and I wouldn't be writing this book if I couldn't add that *but*—I don't think the problems of the career are insurmountable, nor do I think they outweigh its benefits and rewards. Having said that, I must admit that the whole of this chapter is devoted to talk about the potential headaches (some of which are also hazards) that I have come across during my working experience. A heavy chapter? Yes, I agree. But its saving grace, I hope, is that each headache in the list comes with some suggestions for getting through it with fewer aspirins.

FLOOR TIME

As I advised way back in Chapter 5, find out how the floor time is organized (meted out) before you decide to join an office. Among the various methods, I find the half day or the two- to four-hour segment most workable for most people.

You can schedule appointments or errands around the scheduled floor time hours, and while in the office, you can take care of the necessary paperwork that has been piling up in your to-be-done box.

Full days seem to drag on forever. The paperwork gets done, you do some phone canvassing, and then you spend what seems to be a small eternity answering other people's phone calls, writing message slips, and hoping for just a nibble or two at one of the ads in the paper. (The situation is even worse if you are assigned a full day of floor time when there has been no advertising in the previous day's or the morning's paper.) Also the necessity to be in the office for a full day essentially eliminates that day's potential for working with customers or seeking new listing clients.

The rotation on the phone calls method is even worse. You confine yourself to the office in the hope of getting a lead, when, believe it or not, it is the very place where you personally are least likely to generate new business. There is never a guarantee that a call you answer will have a customer on the other end of the line even if you have been sitting in the office for six hours patiently taking your turn at the phone. On the other hand, another agent on the staff may stop in for an hour before going out to dinner with a customer and pick up the one call she answers in her rotation to find a live one on the other end of the line.

WEEKEND DUTY

Generally it is best to try to find an office where you get no more than two weekend days a month. Enough buyers insist on going out on weekends to cut your own weekend leisure time to a minimum without adding the burden of numerous assigned office days. It has been my experience that Saturdays are usually fairly busy and Sundays rather quiet, except in really boom times. So if you like companionship and activity; that is, other agents in and out of the office and lots of phone calls from cooperating offices, choose Saturdays when you can. If, on the other hand, you appreciate a quiet time, choose floor time on Sundays and bring along a good book or a small

TV set to watch your favorite football team or tennis match. Be sure to turn the volume off before you answer the phone, however.

If you are alone in the office on weekend or evening duty, be sure to have the phone number of the nearest police station at your fingertips (or better yet, memorized) in the event of strange or suspicious happenings. And don't be afraid to call. It is better to call the police about some young men you can just make out walking slowly about the rear of the office property as dusk becomes dark and then discover, when the police car arrives with flashing lights, that they are the teenage sons of the people who live in the house whose backyard abuts the office parking lot, and that the boys were picking blackberries, than to wait to see what happens and have that happening turn out to be a robbery or a rape.

CARAVANS AND AGENTS' OPEN HOUSES

There is a point in every real estate woman's career at which houses become boring, especially if you are going to preview or inspect them, rather than show them to customers. But you must go, for nothing increases your effectiveness as an agent more than personal knowledge of a property you are describing.

The most effective way to see the most houses with the least inconvenience is to choose the day or two of the week when the largest number of agents' Open Houses are scheduled, and go to see them as part of an office group (either in one car, or a caravan of cars, depending on the size of your office). Plan the day's tour in a circle to and from the office. Then select and note other new listings that interest you along the route of that circle. Call the owners of those houses unscheduled for inspection and ask for an appointment for a preview inspection by the number of members of the ABC Realty staff in your party.

I have found that the owners of homes not scheduled for Open Houses are usually impressed by the interest of several agents from one office and are willing to cooperate in showing you through their homes, especially if you explain to them how much more effectively an agent can market a property after a personal inspection. (This kind of group expression of interest can also be helpful in picking up expired listings if you keep in touch with the owners of a soon-to-expire house that you inspect.)

Always try to do these pre-inspection tours with at least one full car of agents from your office. This saves gas (you can take turns as to whose car is used) and it gives you the opportunity to discuss the properties professionally among yourselves immediately after each inspection. You can discuss value, special selling points, difficulties, recent comparable sales in the neighborhood, future zoning for the area, new developments proposed for the surrounding open land, or any other information pertinent to the sale of the property, and then make notations of this special information on your listing sheet. Even if no one in your group has a potential customer for a particular house on the tour, the information you share in discussing it may turn out to be very valuable. The next call you take in the office could be a perfect buyer for that very house.

OFFICE MANAGERS

I hate meetings. Yes, they are the most effective way to distribute information to a large group of people. Yes, they do allow working members of the staff to voice their opinions to the management and among their peers. And yes, they are a business necessity. But, so very often meetings get hung up on bickering over a point of immense insignificance and hours of invaluable time are absolutely wasted. This is especially true if the leader of the meeting does not hold the reins tightly. If you find that meetings at your office run on without control, try scheduling showing appointments during meeting times.

I won't win any words of praise from office managers for that last suggestion, but sales agents are always excused from meetings if they have appointments to show property. Then after the meeting get the notes on what happened from the best, and briefest, note taker in the group. If there is something you need to discuss that was brought up at the meeting, make an appointment to talk with your boss about it in private. Your idea will get more attention this way. Also try to persuade the office management to post an agenda of proposed topics of discussion for a meeting a few days before it is to be held. Then you can be sure to be present when something you consider important or controversial is to be discussed.

If, on the other hand, you enjoy meetings, by all means go. Besides getting office information firsthand, you'll have a chance to voice your opinions before your co-workers, and sometimes to talk enthusiastically about a new open listing you just took that everyone should know about and try to show. But for goodness sake, don't let the meeting get hung up on something like who should have which parking place in the yard. If there's a group problem ask that someone or several people be appointed to make up a plan to solve it, and then, at a later meeting, discuss the plan. It is always easier to revise something than to create from scratch.

DAYS OFF

Real ones are hard to get. If you're not careful in the residential sales business you can end up working eight days a week. It's that kind of profession. There are always the buyers who call you at home with a question to be answered, or with a request to go out to see a new house that they just drove by and happened to see another agency's sign on. (You told them about that house a week ago, but they said then that they weren't interested in that part of town!) And there is always the chore that someone wants done yesterday.

Since most agents give up at least part of every weekend, I want to state again that I firmly believe they should have at least one day absolutely *off* during the week. This does *not* mean a day when the agent simply doesn't go into the office, and during which the office answers every phone call for her with, "She's at home today, would you like that number?" That is NOT a day off.

Arrange with your office supervisor to have all calls intercepted and sent to him/her on your day off. Let him solve the problems and answer the questions that require immediate attention (most don't) and let the others pile up on your desk to be handled tomorrow.

Phone calls that come directly to your home are more difficult to handle. Most real estate business cards are printed with the agent's home phone number included, so anyone to whom you have ever given a card can conceivably call you and say, "I just have to see this house today." You will always be tempted to drop everything and run for fear that they mean the "I just *have* to" part and that if you don't show them the house, they will go to someone else who will.

One way to avoid this kind of pressure is to purchase a telephone answering machine, the kind that will record a short message from the caller. Put your phone on machine answering on your days off. Then you can find out who called and sometimes for what, immediately after they hang up. Those people with unimportant requests will usually hang up rather than leave their name and number, and you will still have a record of the people who really want to talk with you. You can answer these calls at your discretion.

If you don't have an answering machine and you are spending your day off at home, try to have someone else in the house answer the phone saying, "I'm sorry, she has the day off today. May I have your name and number and any message?" This works well even with children. They can understand that there is not even the hint of a lie in the statement "She has the day off today." You *do* have the day off even if you are standing next to the phone.

Of course all this is unnecessary if you are simply not at home on your days off. But if you are, and all else fails, don't hesitate to tell your callers, "Today is my day off. Can we make an appointment for tomorrow morning?"

ILLNESS

One of the problems of being an independent contractor (what every real estate salesperson who works solely on a commission basis is) is that there are no "sick days" with pay.

What do you do if you are absolutely debilitated by fever, vomiting, and diarrhea from the local "bug" and someone from the mortgage company calls to say that their appraiser is on his way to do the house you sold last week and the owners are not at home and someone has to be there to let him in or the company will not be able to make a mortgage commitment by the date specified in the contract? Do you drag yourself out of bed and go out to open the door?

Absolutely not! Your office has a stake in every sale you make, most often half of what you make; therefore they also have a stake in supporting that sale. Call your office manager or broker, and tell him/her that you are ill and someone must let the appraiser in. Believe me, someone (perhaps even the broker herself) will.

During longer illnesses, you may have to make arrangements with another sales agent in the office to cover your various deals in progress. In some offices, there is a written policy on how commission money is to be divided in these cases. In other offices, there is a handshake and an "I owe you one" among the agents working together, or an arrangement to pay the covering agent for his/her time if the deal does come to fruition.

Some larger firms also make group health and disability insurance available to their employees, and some local and state Realtor Boards offer group plans with various insurance companies. If you are covered by your husband's company health insurance plan and your family does not depend upon your income as a real estate agent, you probably do not need further health insurance coverage, or you will at least want to weigh the cost of additional coverage against the likelihood of deriving benefits from it.

If, however, you are supporting yourself and possibly a family, you should seriously consider and evaluate the various plans offered by your firm, the Realtor Groups, and private companies that will cover major medical expenses and/or guarantee a monthly income over the course of a long illness or in the case of total disability. Unfortunately, plans that are purchased on an individual rather than a group basis are usually considerably more expensive. And unless your real estate company is particularly large, their group plan will also be more expensive and usually less generous than those currently being offered to employees of America's giant corporations.

MONEY

In his novel *Of Human Bondage,* Somerset Maugham said, "There is nothing so degrading as the constant anxiety about one's means of livelihood. . . . Money is like a sixth sense without which you cannot make a complete use of the other five." How true! Money makes life more beautiful, more harmonious, smoother, tastier, and usually better smelling! And a steady assured supply of it—enough of it, that is—definitely makes living easier and more dignified. But unfortunately I must tell you the sad news (which of course is not news at all) that in real estate sales there is never a steady and assured supply of money. There is no regular weekly or monthly pay check, no tenure, no pension plan after twenty years of service.

If you choose real estate sales as your career, you will receive as your salary only what you earn. Your income will be affected by the socioeconomic status of the area in which you work, the season of the year, the economic health of the nation, the amount of time and effort you put in, your skill and talent, and luck. Some months you may make more than you could possibly spend; others there will be nothing.

If you run a good streak, or if you work very hard and save with particular care, you may make enough extra in six months (or a year, or two years) to begin investing in income-producing properties, using your commissions on those properties as part of the purchase money of course. In this way, you can gradually assure yourself of that elusive steady supply that will get you through the bad times that everyone encounters occasionally in a sales career.

If, on the other hand, you run a bad streak and you do not have other sources of income, you may be forced to consider the company draw. A draw is an advance from the broker (or corporation in the case of the giant firms) on commission you hope to earn when the market is better. It is to be avoided if at all possible, for in taking it, you commit yourself to working in that office with no assurance of when you will earn enough commission to support yourself and wipe out the draw. Think of the American work song that goes: ". . . and I owe my life to the company store." (It's not by accident that *store* almost rhymes with *draw,* especially if you use the proper regional accent.)

If you are a woman working in real estate for the extras in life: to give your children a better education; to take some dream vacations; to buy clothes that are a little nicer; to enjoy dining in the finest restaurants once in a while; to live in a nicer home of your own; to get an inside lead on investment properties; and/or all the other more beautiful, tastier, smoother joys, the irregularity of commissions will affect you but little. You are among the more fortunate of our profession, and I have just two warnings for you:

One, don't forget Uncle Sam. Since no money is withheld from commissions for federal income taxes, you must be aware of how your earnings will affect your annual taxable income. Some families handle this problem by guessing at the wife's annual income and then taking a larger withholding from the husband's income to compensate, hoping that the totals come out more or less even at the end of the year. Other families file an estimated quarterly tax payment based on the real estate agent's projected earnings.

And two, don't spend any commission money before you have it in hand. I have seen deals fall apart the day before closing, and lots of them fall apart long before that. When they do, there is no pay for your work. If you have already spent that expected money, you will have to work to make it up, and when you get paid for the next sale, you will find it less rewarding. The excitement will be gone because the new commission check will be committed to paying back what you spent from the deal that didn't happen. Nothing is more disheartening and anxiety provoking than working in a commission-based career and trying always to pay back what was already spent.

If you are a woman supporting yourself and a family on the income of your real estate career, or if the additional income from your work is essential to your family's economic well-being, you must be more aware of the uncertainties and fluctuations of commission income and more careful in allocating it throughout the entire year.

"That sounds almost like an accounting job," you say. "Where do I start? What do I do?"

It's really not very complicated. As a first step, ask your broker and/or your local Realtor Board about statistics on the average and median incomes for sales agents, both beginning and experienced, in your area. Ask if there are any charts available showing the number of sales on your MLS in each month of the year. Your own income will probably, at first anyway, be on the low side of the median and it will probably closely follow the peaks and valleys pattern of area sales. (In most areas, this is best in spring and worst in December.)

Then on separate sheets of paper, make some charts of your own outlining your family's financial needs over the course of a year. Where are the greatest demands for money? When? Don't forget heating costs, insurance payments, school clothes, vacations, etc. When are the easy times? How much did your family spend last year? How much will they probably need this year? Then break that down into how much they will probably need in each individual month.

As your fiscal year begins and your commission checks start to come in, check off the basic needs of the month they support, and put the extra in the bank toward the needs of the year as a whole. Do this for each month until you have enough in the bank to be certain that you can get through the whole year. Then you can start buying the extras, planning the big vacation, or looking for good investments.

And again, don't forget Uncle Sam. Talk with a good accountant and learn how to file quarterly tax returns.

Besides no federal income tax deductions, there will also be no social security contributions deducted from your commission checks. However, as a self-employed person; that is, one who works as an independent contractor on a commission basis, you are still responsible for social security contributions on your net income after deductions. You must pay this social security contribution, called *the self-employment tax*, with your annual income tax. The rules and procedures are outlined in the Internal Revenue Service booklet titled *Tax Guide for Small Businesses* (Publication #334). As a contributor to the social security system, you are also entitled to its benefits.

The government also has established a plan which allows self-employed persons to contribute untaxed income annually towards their retirement security. The rules and procedures of this plan, called an Individual Retirement Account, are discussed in detail in the Internal Revenue Service booklet titled *Your Federal Income Tax* (Publication #17). It is available free of charge from the IRS office in your area.

Every woman working in real estate, whether full time or part time, whether for extras or for her livelihood, should take the time to discuss the benefits of an Individual Retirement Account with a good accountant. The temptation is always to spend extra money. But putting it aside for the future may actually add to your spendable income. How? The magic words are "tax shelter." For example, in a given fiscal year, your Individual Retirement Account contribution might just edge you into a lower tax bracket!

DISPUTES BETWEEN SALESPEOPLE

When each person working in an office is an independent contractor and paid by earned commission, there are bound to be occasional disputes. Did that couple walk into the office at 11:59 or 12 Noon? The exact time would determine whose customers they would be if the floor-time assignment changed at noon. Does the lady who calls the office and says, "I'd like some information about the sales prices of houses on Franklin Terrace" and leaves her name with the agent who answered the phone belong to that agent as a potential listing customer? Think about this. Especially if she meets another agent from the same office at a cocktail party two months later and signs the house up with the new agent despite the fact that the original agent had made two visits to the property and called the woman three times during those two months. How would you decide? And if you were the agent decided against, how would you react?

In most cases disputes between sales agents are settled by the broker or office manager. Some offices have extensive written policy manuals that try to anticipate all possible situations and decree their settlement. In other offices, the broker just listens and decides, or sometimes negotiates a settlement between the two parties. A few larger firms actually have mediation panels, where officers of the company and appointed sales agent representatives hear problems.

In cases where an agent feels she has been decided against wrongly or is unwilling to accept the compromise offered, she can usually appeal to the grievance committee of the Realtor Board to which the broker belongs. If he is not a member of a Realtor Board, or if she objects also to the decision of the Board, she can sometimes, depending upon the situation and circumstances, take her grievance to the State Real Estate Commission and request a hearing. It is a messy, time- and energy-consuming process, however, and most agents find it better to try to solve problems by a compromise than to pursue an "I'm absolutely right" course to the bitter end.

DISPUTES WITH YOUR BROKER

When a sales agent has not been properly paid or when she feels that some aspect of her working agreement with her broker has been violated, she can again appeal to the grievance committee of the Realtor Board; or if that fails to bring results or if the option is not available to her, she may also go to the State Real Estate Commission. It is always best, however, if the agent has a written contract of employment upon which to base her complaint. I cannot stress strongly enough how important it is to have a working agreement before you start working. Many Realtor Boards have printed employment forms available and most of the large companies have their own, usually with considerably more specific clauses and restrictions.

No matter what type of written contract you are offered, however, be sure to read it carefully. Do not hesitate to question anything you do not understand or feel uneasy about. Do not accept "Oh, that's just printed in there. It never happens" as a rationalization for anything. If it never happens, have the clause struck out. If you request any special allowances and the management agrees to them during your interview, have them written into your contract. No, I'm not being picky. Mutual agreements in writing usually assure fair treatment if and when a problem does arise.

And, finally, if you feel the least bit uncertain about the contract you are about to sign, if there is any clause in it that you do not understand fully or that you wish to have worded differently, please, for your future peace of mind, take a few hours, call your attorney, and ask him/her to review it with you.

DISPUTES WITH CUSTOMERS OR CLIENTS

When people are playing a high-risk game which as often as not involves their life savings, they sometimes complain vociferously if they think they have lost or scored poorly, especially if they can conjure up even the slightest hint of unfair play. And a cry of "Foul!" can bring you into court.

Court cases demand time, which in the residential sales business can be translated directly into money lost. So one of your prime objectives while playing in this high-risk, high-reward game, is never to be charged with misconduct.

We both know the next question. How? Well, when it comes to legal complaints, written records are your lifeline. The two most common areas of complaint are money and misrepresentation. Let's start with money.

Whenever you receive escrow or earnest money from a buyer, give him/her a receipt, even if the money is in the form of a check. Then turn that check over to your broker immediately, or as immediately as possible, and get a receipt from him/her. If your broker balks at giving you a receipt for every deposit check that you bring in, type up a form which you can run through the copy machine and present it with each deposit. It should read something like:

Mr. Broker:

check
Attached is a cash in the amount of ________ which I received from ______________ as an earnest money deposit with their offer of _________ for the property located at ______________ and owned by ______________. Please deposit and hold this sum in your trust account pending the outcome of negotiation on this property.

____________________	______________________________
DATE	YOUR NAME
	Received and accepted by
	______________________________
	YOUR BROKER'S NAME

It will take but a few minutes of your time to fill in the blanks on this form, but it will protect you from blame if money is lost or unaccounted for.

Now to misrepresentation. If there are problems in a house that you are aware of, point them out to the buyers and if possible include a line on the offer form or contract that reads something like: "Mr. & Mrs. Buyer are aware that water has seeped into the basement of this property on several occasions during the past year"; or "Mr. & Mrs. Buyer are aware of proposed plans for a highway to be built sometime within the next five years that would pass within 100 yards of this property." This type of statement will prevent you from being taken to court because "The agent never told us about . . ."

Another protective device is to suggest the use of a professional home inspection service. Recommend that your buyers make the contract contingent upon an acceptable report from the service. This brings in a third, disinterested party to testify to the soundness of the property. Do not, however, neglect to mention any problems of which you are aware simply because there is a home inspection service on the job. The inspection service does not relieve you of your responsibility for fair conduct and honesty.

If you are working with shaky buyers (financially), inform your sellers. A line such as "Mr. & Mrs. Seller have been informed that Mr. & Mrs. Buyer may not qualify for a mortgage in the amount of $________, and Mr. & Mrs. Seller are willing to enter into this contract provided that the mortgage contingency clause expire three weeks from this date and not be extended beyond that day" can be added to a contract and initialed by all parties concerned. It protects you from being accused of bringing unqualified buyers to the property. Misrepresenting unqualified buyers as qualified could cause a house to be tied up and off the market for several weeks. This makes sellers very unhappy, and they become positively furious if really qualified buyers appear during this period and cannot or do not buy the house because it is off the market waiting for the mortgage commitment of your shaky buyers.

To protect yourself when negotiating, try to get all relevant facts on paper every time you go back and forth between the buyers and sellers, along with their signatures and initials where necessary, of course. This is important to avoid your getting caught in a situation where Mr. Seller says, "She told *me* . . ." and Mr. Buyer says, "Oh, no! She told *me* . . ." It is absolutely essential that everything is clear and aboveboard when negotiating and the more you can get written down the better. And keep and file all the papers (even the telephone messages) involved in the transaction with the dates clearly marked on each.

If your customers or clients do file suit, the suit will most often be against both you and your employing broker since the broker is responsible for the actions of his or her sales agents. Most brokers have been through several legal actions of one kind or another during their careers and have contact with attorneys competent in handling these cases. Rely on the judgment of your broker in this case and follow the advice of the attorney he suggests. Usually the broker will split the attorney's fee with you, but ask who pays the fee at the outset, and get the agreement in writing if you can.

DRIVING HAZARDS

Most agents drive their prospective buyers from house to house. Occasionally some buyers want to go out in the most incredible weather or at the most difficult times—5 o'clock rush hour, for example. If it bothers you to drive on a particular day or under particular circumstances, simply ask if they can make their appointment at another time. Driving scared or nervous is a very quick road to an accident.

So is driving blind. If you can possibly find the time, try to run over your routes before you have your buyers in the car. It is quite easy to become involved in an accident when you are hunting for house numbers, talking to your buyers about the excellent school down the street, and steering the car all at the same time.

And it may sound elementary, but I can't leave this particular hazard without reminding you again that you should check to be sure that your car insurance is adequate. Some companies have higher rates if you use your car for business purposes, but you must have the insurance protection. (And the extra cost for business use insurance is tax deductible.)

But talk with a good agent. Or better yet talk with several agents. Ask a lot of questions and compare their answers.

OPEN HOUSES, EMPTY HOUSES, AND LATE NIGHT NEGOTIATING

A newspaper article that I read several years ago significantly affected my ideas about good working habits in the residential sales business. It was titled "Thieves Posing As Home Buyers: It's Hard to Prevent" and, quite literally, it scared me. Let me run a few examples by you and see if it doesn't scare you, too:

Linda Stillson, a broker in Hialeah, Fla., was raped and beaten to death in a vacant townhouse 22 miles outside Pensacola.

Patty Kerger, a 28-year-old associate broker in Phoenix, Ariz., had a 5 P.M. appointment to show a $100,000 townhouse. Her body was found in a vacant lot. She had been struck on the head and stabbed.

Lois Higbie, 54, of Milbourne, Fla., was killed by stabbing when she met a man prospect in an empty house. A similar fate befell an Oklahoma woman. And in Palatine, Ill., Stephanie Ann Lyng left for a property showing and has never been found.

Characteristically, none of these crimes has been solved. There have been some narrow escapes, too. An Indianapolis saleswoman, showing a prospect through a condominium, got away from her attacker only by jumping through a first-floor plate-glass window.

"There definitely is a certain type of psychopath who looks on women real estate agents as fair game," says police chief Stanley Gontarz of Barrington, R.I. He has acquired a specialized knowledge of the subject. Over the last seven years he has been following tips from throughout the country trying to break the only unsolved murder in his career of more than a decade as chief. That was the strangling of Mrs. Teri Macdonald on April 30, 1971, in the basement of an empty house. The "prospect" who killed this broker had scouted not only her office but several others before selecting his victim.

Is that enough? Are you ready to look for a job in a good shoe store? Don't. Not yet anyway. The stories are terrifying, yes, but when you realize that there are more than 754,000 members of the National Association of Realtors in this country and that 51 percent of that number are women—women who show houses and condos and empty land every day—the stories of violence come into perspective. Statistically there is probably no more violence in the real estate profession than among nurses who work the night shift, or waitresses, or newspaper reporters, or social workers, or any other profession where women have unusual hours or are alone when they leave the shelter of their homes and offices.

My point in leading you through these horror stories, however, is that there are some situations inherent to a real estate career that are indeed potentially dangerous. And there are some techniques which you should know to minimize the danger.

May I first recommend a very fine paperback book by police captain James A. Smith called *Rapists Beware* (Collier Books, 1978)? It should be read not only by real estate agents, but by every woman who goes anywhere alone. Captain Smith discusses and depicts numerous techniques and tools of self defense. Those that impressed me as most important for real estate agents are keys and magazines.

"A woman is very vulnerable when standing at her car door, searching her purse for her keys," says Captain Smith. He suggests that you always have your keys in your hand before leaving a building and he discusses how to use those keys in your own defense if you are attacked. In brief, a metal key is a pointed weapon. It can be directed toward eyes, throat, or ribs, and it can pierce with enough force to stun and seriously injure an attacker.

Magazines, believe it or not, can also become powerful pointed weapons. Captain Smith suggests that you roll an ordinary magazine so that only one end comes to a sharp point. He recommends that you then grasp the rolled magazine about two to three inches from the point and use it to strike with force if threatened. He says that a magazine so rolled and used will break a 1 x 6-inch wooden board, and he points out that the weapon can be used against any part of the attacker's body that is vulnerable: groin, temples, eyes, windpipe, forehead, stomach, kidneys, and even the back of his hands which are especially sensitive and full of small breakable bones. Captain Smith stresses that "Carrying a magazine should become a habit for a woman, and she ought to practice rolling it quickly and striking out with it in all directions. A magazine should be at hand in the front seat of an automobile and in every room of the home."

Now you know that you're not going to find a magazine in every room of an empty house that you're showing. But you might carry one. A professional publication with photos of area houses does not look out of place. You might also carry throughout the house the key that you removed from the lock box rather than return it to the box after opening the door. You will of course then have to re-open the box to return that key, but by then you can gracefully and unobtrusively be holding your car keys.

Naturally you do not need to follow these precautions with well-established customers, but on the first time out it's certainly a good idea to be on the over-cautious side, even if your customer resembles a Fortune 500 executive.

Check out the home addresses that customers give you in a phone book or city directory if these tools are available to you before you go out on a showing appointment. If a prospect says he is from out of town ask for his street address, then call Directory Assistance in that town and ask for his phone number. If a prospect represents himself as an employee of a local company, call him back there on some pretense such as changing the time by fifteen minutes or so. But don't use the direct-line number that he gave you; go through the company switchboard in order to be certain that you are in fact reaching the company he named.

It is also a good idea to avoid empty or especially secluded houses on the first time out. And never agree to meet a new prospective buyer at a property or in a parking lot. A customer's willingness to come into your office and be seen by the other members of the office staff is at least some assurance of safety. Stop at the secretary's desk as you go out and say "I'm taking Mr. Stevens to see the properties on High Street and Circle Drive. We should be back within an hour if there are any calls for me."

Sunday floor time, when you are often alone in the office, is more difficult. Walk-ins are often good customers, anxious to buy. But there is also always the very remote chance that they might be thieves or psychopaths looking for access into a house they might rob or for a woman they might rape. At the very least, call the answering service before you leave an empty office to show houses on Sunday and say, "This is Sally Wyndham speaking. I'm assigned to floor time today, but I will be taking Mr. Peter Stark out to see some property for about an hour. Will you please leave a note for Mr. Broker that I will be showing Mr. Stark 14 Maple Street and 29 Windy Hill Road."

But if you have any doubt or negative feelings at all about that Sunday afternoon walk-in, simply say, "I'm sorry, but I'm the only one on duty at this moment, although other agents do usually check in from time to time. If you would like to wait until another member of our staff arrives, I could try to arrange for some showings. Or perhaps you would like to go through our Multiple Listing books and choose those properties that most appeal to you. Then we could talk about the costs of carrying various properties and choose those most suitable to you and your family. This would save considerable time, and we could arrange to see the houses you most prefer tomorrow or whatever day is convenient for you."

This kind of delaying action keeps you in the relative safety of the office and gives you a chance to gather more information about the prospective buyer and even perhaps to qualify him. If he is on the up-and-up, he should give you the information you request (which you can verify after he leaves or during the following day). If he is not, he will probably beat a hasty retreat and try another real estate office.

Probably the biggest single change that the "Thieves Posing As Home Buyers" article effected in my attitude toward real estate practices concerns public Open Houses. Follow my thinking if you will: Once I put out the sign that invites everyone or anyone to come in, I say good-by to the owners and stand completely alone in the house with no control over the flow of traffic through it. In most cases I have never before seen the people who enter and have no way of verifying the names they mumble to me.

Theoretically thieves could work in groups: one couple or "family" to keep me busy talking while the other searches the house for valuables or cases the joint for a break-in on another day. And in the case of a particularly secluded house, what's to stop a man, or group of men, from locking the door behind them after they enter the house? I know, it certainly doesn't happen very often, but once is too many times. If you must hold Open Houses, try to work in pairs or groups.

Late night negotiating is another potential real estate hazard, but one that I have not been able to avoid. When bids are going back and forth, and closing dates, mortgage contingencies, extras, and points are being traded off, you can't say, "Let's stop for the evening, I like to be home by 9:30." You stay with the job until it is finished. But park your car in a well-lighted place, have the keys ready before you leave the building, and check the back seat before you get in. Finally, don't return to the closed and empty office to drop off the earnest money check and the signed contracts. If you finished negotiating at 11:09 P.M., you can certainly keep the contract and the check in your possession until 9 A.M. the following morning. Go home and sleep well.

At the beginning of this chapter I promised you some suggestions for needing fewer aspirins, but I suspect you may have needed a couple to get through reading all this. Perhaps I shouldn't have gathered all the headaches into one chapter; in reality they are dispersed over a great deal of time and some of them never touch an individual agent during the entire course of her career. Yes, residential real estate has some headaches, dry drudgery, and hazards, but there are many, many good days and good times that counterbalance the cost of aspirin. And with these particular headaches, like most of life's problems, once you recognize and get to know them, you are well on your way to being able to manage them.

ELEVEN

A Woman First

IT WAS early Saturday evening. I had been out showing houses all day, I was tired, and my feet hurt. Mechanically, without enthusiasm, I changed into a fresh pair of pantyhose and pulled a midnight-blue velvet dress over my head. The zipper stuck, halfway, exactly in that place where your arms can't quite reach from top or bottom. I swore with frustration and attacked the cloth and metal teeth again. Somewhere along the course of the upward struggle I thought, "Why am I doing this? I don't want to go to this party. The Youngs are moving to Arizona. I'll probably never see them again and I've already contacted everyone else who'll be there. There's not a single prospect in the whole evening."

There's not a single prospect in the whole evening. Almost as I thought them, the words came back to startle me. What was I saying! The Youngs had been good friends for five years and this was their farewell party. Everyone who would be there was a friend or neighbor of long standing, people I had worked with, and shared interests with, and chauffered children with. Yet I had lumped them all together into prospects.

It was a moment of truth, a realization that forced me to stop fighting the zipper a minute and think. Had my career so taken over my life that I judged everything in terms of it? Was there no person named Carolyn left who loved her family, and her friends, and a good time just for what they were? Had listings and customers and sales come to mean more to me than what I had always thought most precious?

I shook my head and told myself, "You're just tired. It was just a weak moment." And I finished zipping the dress.

It may indeed have been a weak moment, or an angry one, but it was a moment vivid enough to remain in my memory for over nine years now. It was the moment I realized that in this highly competitive business, I and I alone must draw the line between work and leisure.

But why the fuss? Was I especially ambitious? Especially in love with the real estate game to let it gain twenty-four-hour-a-day priority? Not at all. In fact I have discovered that what happened to me as I struggled with that sticky zipper happens at some point to almost every woman who actively pursues success in this career. The business slowly pervades your life.

Since buying and selling houses is a part of most people's lives at some time or other, it is a topic of discussion at cocktail parties, and coffees, and nursery school picnics, and Newcomers Club luncheons, and bridge groups, and gourmet dinner club gatherings, and in Little League and Soccer Club parking lots, and supermarket aisles, and beauty parlor waiting rooms. And yes, I did tell you that all these places were good spots to meet prospects and further business. And yes, I did tell you to let people know that you were a real estate agent and to speak up about your opinions and knowledge. But somewhere you must also draw a line between furthering your business and following your interests. The motivation for joining a recreational group should be recreation. If that recreation brings in leads (which it probably will), all well and good, but don't go to the club meeting, or tennis match, or PTA committee, or whatever, for the prospects. Go for the fun. Everyone needs some fun just for the sake of fun in her life.

But enough moralizing and theory. Let's get down to the logistics of the problem. How do you put boundaries on a job that has the potential of permeating every minute of a twenty-four-hour day? (I'm including the sleepless nights everyone occasionally suffers through when involved in red-hot negotiation.)

Well, I've already mentioned days off, and you *should* take them. But you should also schedule hours off—times when you simply don't take calls, when you are busy with the necessities of being the person you are.

"But how?" you ask. "How does one find the time and take it?"

At the risk of boring you, I'll tell you one more personal story in response. I am a person who scored below the 15th percentile in a high school test of clerical skills some twenty-five years ago. The test results shocked me. Eighty-five percent of the world was better than I was at keeping records and filing. Pretty bad, right? And yes, you guessed it, I still can't keep my desk drawers neat, and my files are coded under a secret system which only I understand (put the letter in the first open folder), and there are still piles of things-to-be-done in the most inappropriate places around my work area. But, and I mean this sincerely, I have learned during the past twenty-five years to respect those skills that I have never completely mastered. And I advise you to learn to organize and schedule, for the time spent learning and using these skills will come back tenfold in free time that you may use to develop and enjoy your other skills and interests. In the real estate game, structure can give you freedom by locking out business when and where business doesn't belong.

CALENDARS

Organizing time is of course more difficult than organizing things, since time just won't stand still. So at the very beginning of your career buy and keep two kinds of calendars, a large month-at-a-glance type on or near your desk with floor-time schedules, closing dates, and days off clearly marked in the squares, and a book type that will fit into your briefcase but provides ample space for each day, broken down into lines for each hour or half hour. On the second calendar, fill in those long-term firm dates such as closings at the appropriate hour, but then plan the unscheduled time of each day as you come to it.

I know you're still saying to yourself, "But that takes time."

And I am still responding, "Not as much time as it saves."

If each evening you take a few minutes to plan the coming day, you will work more efficiently, save recrossing your own tracks, and come out less fatigued and more successful. You will learn to take the time for recreation, the time to re-create your energies.

If, however, you don't schedule your own time, you will find that it will be scheduled for you. You will become a fire fighter, always running to put out a blaze here or investigate smoke there. Your life will then be governed by the demands and needs of others, which is probably the most fatiguing of all possible life-styles. Time is the only resource that everyone possesses equally; none of us has more than twenty-four hours in one day. But time *management* is not equal. You must plan and work so that your needs will play a major role in determining your time management.

Again I can hear you thinking. This time you are saying to yourself, "That's a very nice statement in print, but it just doesn't work. I have a husband and three kids, or a dependent parent, or a demanding boss, or customers who will leave for another agent if they don't get the service they want when they want it, or obligations in several organizations that depend upon me, or friends who need me, or . . ." You name it. And it's true; everyone has responsibilities. But the responsibilities that you take on and the manner in which you choose to fill those responsibilities are responses to your needs too. The secret to real success—not just financial success but living success (that is living a life that is satisfying to you)—is recognizing your own needs and then organizing your life in a way that allows you to fulfill as many of those needs as possible.

Your career is one of those needs. You are considering or have chosen a career in real estate because of some need that you have, perhaps it is a need to get out of the house, or to have an identity and income of your own, or perhaps to meet financial obligations. Whatever it is, it is one of your needs, but it certainly cannot be all of your needs. So I come back to the zipper story, and the realization that a career cannot and should not determine your life. Put it and its needs along with your other needs in their proper perspective.

This is all, of course, more easily said than done. But I won't leave you here. Let's look at women in some specific life situations, some fictional real people as it were, and see how real estate sales fits into their lives. Remember the real estate luncheon mural that I painted in Chapter 2? I'd like to go back to it now and choose some of those women for full-length portraits. What's happening in their lives and how is each managing to fit the job in? What are the specific time demands and the peculiar stresses of each, and how has each woman learned to cope? In examining each of them you may learn much about your career and perhaps something about yourself.

DORIS

Doris, the woman in the silver-blue wool suit who was the speaker at the luncheon, is a graduate of Vassar College and the wife of a prominent local dentist. Her three children are grown, the youngest girl just having graduated from college.

Doris has been in real estate for nine years and has all the qualifications required in her state for a broker's license. She has not, however, taken the examination for that license, nor will she. Doris intends to remain in sales. She does not want the responsibilities nor the time demands of managing an office or starting her own firm. In fact, she chose her job in sales carefully, knowing well its requirements, limitations, and rewards.

Until her youngest child entered junior high school, Doris had devoted herself to her home and family and a few selected community activities, but at that point in her family's growth and in her own life she became restless and dissatisfied. Despite the financial security of her family, she wanted to pursue a career in her own right. She chose real estate because of its freedom and flexible hours and because she felt she could learn enough in the field to become a strong voice in the newly formed movement to rejuvenate the city in which she lived. She also hoped to work through professional channels toward more adequate housing for low-income families. At the time that we see her in our mural she is respected for her competence and contributions in both the local and statewide real estate communities.

Doris's career has not moved along a straight and smooth road over those nine years, however. She began work with a small independent Realtor of excellent reputation, and she did well in sales and rentals, but as her professional and community activities increased, she found it more and more difficult to keep abreast of the market, and to handle efficiently the paperwork required in her job. She also resented weekend showings and found it difficult to leave her customers and deals-in-progress for the five to seven weeks of vacation she and her husband took each year.

Doris solved some of her problems by transferring her license to one of the largest multi-office brokers in the state. Because of the large staff of sales agents in her office, floor time there was minimal, with very few weekend commitments. Secretarial assistants and mortgage specialists took over most of the paperwork which she had so often found bothersome.

Working in this new office, Doris tried to schedule most of her showings on weekdays, but she never could completely eliminate the necessity of some weekend work. Instead she made a self-imposed ruling to limit showings to *one* day of each weekend. Occasionally she lost a customer because of her work style, but her rules kept her career in a workable balance with her commitment to her marriage and social life. She worked out the problem of frequent vacations by accepting less commission on the transactions that required the office manager's personal attention while she was away.

Doris did not enter real estate for the money to be made there, although her yearly income eventually became quite substantial. She entered it as a challenge, a place to use her knowledge and leadership skills and as a place in which she could contribute to the growth and improvement of her community. She found satisfaction for all these needs in the career, along with the bonus of often bringing home the ingredients for truly interesting and amusing dinner-table tales and conversation with her husband. She is happy in her work and has no plans for a career change.

JOYCE

Joyce is the dark-haired woman in the center of the mural speaking to Doris. In dress, manner, refinement, even appearance, they look somewhat alike, but their stories are very different.

Joyce was divorced eleven years ago at age forty-one. The settlement was generous, her husband openly admitted his affair with another woman. Joyce kept the house and custody of their two high-school-age children and was awarded both child support and alimony that seemed more than adequate. But there was no provision in the legal papers for her total disorientation, her torn and crushed sense of self.

Joyce had dropped out of college in her sophomore year to marry her husband. She moved smoothly from being someone's daughter to being someone's wife and then someone's mother. Twenty years later, however, she discovered that she was an adult woman, alone, without unmarried friends, without what the employment agencies called marketable skills, and without self-confidence. She spent her first four sessions in therapy crying.

But three, perhaps four months later, the therapist showed her a door, and urged her to open it. It was a door he had chosen intuitively and for all the wrong reasons, but at least it was a door. They had been talking about Joyce's interests and the therapist had pointed out that they all centered on home crafts and decorating. He suggested that she look into selling residential real estate, a career that many women picked up in mid-life, that required minimal previous formal education, that would give her a chance to develop her interest in decorating, and that would get her out meeting people again. In theory, it sounded like the ideal solution, and Joyce signed up for a salesman's licensing course.

The course and the examination were the easy part; the rocky road started afterward. Joyce joined a large franchised office and discovered that decorating had nothing to do with selling, and that she knew nothing about selling. She went through all the sales training courses that were offered and passed with flying colors. But it was different the moment she got outside the classroom, into the real world.

Joyce found it difficult to ask for listings or offers, and very difficult to say "no" to any customer request. She found the required canvassing nearly impossible, a literal mental torture since her sense of worthlessness increased with each rejection, which she took as rejections of herself. She agonized over negotiating, taking personal blame for every deal that fell apart. And, finally, almost a year later, she stood up one day and screamed at her therapist that there was nothing, *nothing* she could do well.

They talked a long time that day, far past the limits of the hour session. He told her it was important that she not give up her job at this point and urged her to give it one more try in another atmosphere. The therapist knew two brokers who ran independent one-office firms. Joyce shook her head; she wanted to get out entirely. But then she stopped, almost in mid-thought, and looked up. The view on the other side of quitting loomed up at her and looked so dismal that she nodded and chose the chance at one more try.

And she was lucky. Joyce interviewed both brokers and chose the one who required no canvassing and seemed easier to talk with. He was. He carefully walked her through deal after deal, pointing out and interpreting what was happening behind the scenes, and why and how she could handle the situations both professionally and personally. Over the course of the first six months, he repeated again and again that there were many factors in each situation that she could not control or affect, and that her responsibility was to be honest and efficient, nothing more.

Success came slowly, but it came, each completed transaction building a foundation of security. In her fourth year as a sales agent, Joyce made the Million Dollar Club. There were other rewards, too. As she worked, she developed a network of unmarried friends with whom she could enjoy a busy social life. She joined the Woman's Council of Realtors where she found support for herself, and where she found that she could give support to others.

Joyce was never bothered by the odd hours and weekend work of a real estate career, especially after both her children left for college. Somehow working filled the empty places and gave her purpose. And she met men, other real estate agents mostly, but also lawyers, bankers, mortgage representatives, buyers. Sometimes there were open advances which she learned to deal with courteously while keeping her professional status, and once, for a while, there had been a relationship with a newly divorced lawyer. But that was over and she had survived it well. Joyce at fifty-two was a professional success and a busy woman.

EVELYN

Evelyn is painted sitting at the table, talking with animation and control. She had once been a high school prom queen and a runner-up in the Miss Pennsylvania pageant. Everywhere at that time there had been the same chorus: She would be a model. Black was in, there were lots of jobs, and she was so beautiful.

Evelyn found an apartment with two roommates (they were each nineteen), and yes, she began to find jobs. But it was not at all like the castles she had built sitting on her bed with her friends on those sunny Saturday afternoons when she was sixteen.

The work was not glamorous, but hard and often boring, hours at a time of repeating pose after pose to the clicking cameras. The competition was incredible. She was always a number, an applicant, judged for her body, or her face, or her hands, or her smile. No one ever seemed to ask about Evelyn the whole person. And there were many intervals when there simply was no work.

During one of the tough times, she answered another kind of ad. *Real estate sales agents wanted. Flexible hours, high income potential, we'll train you.* She hoped to earn only enough to pay her share of the rent and perhaps have a little money for fun. And she hoped the job would leave plenty of time to allow her to keep and build her modeling career.

But Evelyn got hooked. She got her real estate license and she discovered that she was good at selling condos and co-ops and at finding just the right tenants for a sublet. And she discovered that she liked it! She liked being in a world where she made decisions, she liked having responsibility, and she liked a commission income which could go up when she worked harder.

Evelyn couldn't help but notice that people were attracted to her by her beauty, and then sometimes hesitant or even condescending because of her youth and femininity. But she learned to expect these reactions, and to deal with them. She worked to be best, and she elicited—no, commanded—respect for her knowledge and competence within shorter and shorter periods of working time with each new customer or client. And she liked that. She liked being a person, not a photographic object. She let her modeling career dribble away and enrolled in a local GRI (Graduate Realtor Institute) course of study as a stepping stone to her own standard of excellence.

There were men in her life, but right now, as the mural is painted, she has no one man. Evelyn wants a career and a good one. She wants freedom, and respect and recognition, and some of life's luxuries. And she is willing to work for it all. Her sights are set on a broker's license, and then her own office, and then perhaps offices. She intends to do it all before marriage and a family, and then if marriage and a family become a part of her life, she intends to keep her business too. She sees real estate as a business she will be able to keep.

CLAIRE

Claire is seated next to Evelyn at the table. It was just over four years ago that the phone rang to change her life. *There had been an accident on Route 36. Could she come to the hospital immediately?* Her husband died the following day.

There was no will, some insurance, and a great many frightening questions. They had one child, a boy, thirteen.

Claire had worked in clothing stores and was working at the time of the accident as a bank teller, but she saw quickly that she and her son could not live comfortably on that income, even with the help of insurance and social security. A friend of her husband's suggested that Claire might like to try working in his office as a real estate agent.

The idea startled her at first. That was high-powered stuff, competitive, commissions, sales pressure, legal problems. It seemed too big for her. But the friend persisted. He invited Claire to his office and explained its workings and the demands of the sales job to her. He had faith in her, he said, he felt she could handle it. There was enough insurance to carry her through a couple years if necessary, and if she needed a draw against future commissions ever, he would provide it. The realistic potential income, he explained, was almost double that of her job as a bank teller.

Claire decided to give it a try, thinking that she could always go back to being a bank teller, but the try was very successful. She learned quickly, and learned to have confidence in her opinions and her knowledge. She was a very open, giving, and honest person, and customers sensed her sincerity and stayed with her. She often got referrals and she was building a reputation for good service and dependability.

Her problems were not with the work, but with the very nature of the profession. She worried about her teenage son who was so often left home alone. He seemed reliable and stable, and yet there was always the question in her mind. She called him (perhaps too often) from appointments that ran over, and when she was at home they talked together often. The talking helped. His father's death had changed the boy, made him more mature and more sensitive, but also more cautious and in many ways more dependent. Claire told herself again and again that he would be fine, but she knew she would always worry about him a little, probably even after he was off on his own. Right now the strange hours, the weekend work, the drop-everything-and-run calls made the worry a little worse.

Then there was the money, too. Yes, she was making much more than even her best hopes for promotion at the bank would have brought her, but it was never secure, never regular. There was always the temptation to splurge in those months when the commission checks were plentiful, and there was always the shadow of fear in the lean months.

Claire had to learn about health insurance plans, and life insurance, and car insurance, and retirement plans. She had to learn about federal taxes and quarterly returns. She had to learn about investing. And sometimes the "had to's" seemed huge and intimidating. But she learned to take them a step at a time and to lean unselfconsciously on friends when an arm was offered.

She also had to adjust to living in an entirely different lifestyle. As a single parent solely responsible for her own support and the support of her child, she was motivated by need and she sometimes even felt the tugs of ambition, feelings she had never experienced as a wife. Work was always there beckoning to her to come in and in and in, and tempting her with the promise of rewards.

Claire found it hard to stop to smell the flowers. It was much easier to forget herself, and even sometimes her son, and respond to the demands that grew to crowd everything else out of each hour.

Her husband's friend, now of course her friend and broker, stepped in again. He knew how her job could turn into an insatiable monster, and he began talking with her about it. He insisted that she take days off and he showed her how to work daily and weekly schedules.

Sometimes it was easy, sometimes not. But gradually Claire became very much aware of her needs and insecurities, and of the temptation to overcompensate. She was working on the problem. She was learning to see herself as an important person and to make time for that person.

SUSAN

The blond woman, sitting with Evelyn and Claire, is Susan. Susan wishes she could gain some weight, have a better figure, and stop smoking, and she filled her fourth prescription for Librium before coming to the luncheon.

If you had told Susan two years ago that she would be a real estate agent now, she would have laughed. "I'm a secretary," she would have said, "and a damn good one, too!" And she was.

When she took her job at Hearthside Realty, the office seemed to be running on luck and paper clips. Within three months, it was well organized and neat. The listings were up to date, the closed deals file and sales pending file were in perfect order, and all the schedules and letters were typed neatly and on time. The phone was answered courteously and competently, and business was definitely improving.

The credit fell quite rightly to Susan. Her boss said she was much too good to be a secretary and urged her to get her real estate license so that she could really be a part of the office activity and make some big money, too. Susan took the idea home to her husband saying, "I don't think I want to do it." But her husband saw it as a promotion, an opportunity, and added his urging to that of her boss.

Susan got her license and began selling. She knew much about the business already, so her training time as an agent was short and she made some impressive sales and took several good listings rather quickly.

But she was tired, always tired. Susan began to feel that her job never ended, had no limits. She kept trying to get negotiations and deals in order, and nothing would *stay* in order. There were problems, always problems, and things just didn't, wouldn't, fit where they should fit. She found herself working to catch up on paperwork at night, and she found herself doing the tasks that the buyers, or sellers, or lawyers, or bankers neglected or were slow to accomplish. And she worried always if she had done enough, if she had done the negotiating properly, if she had forgotten anything, if she had neglected anyone. She was making an excellent income, she was hailed as a good agent, and she hated the work.

Sitting at that luncheon table, Susan was only half listening to Evelyn talk about the opportunities for women in real estate. She was wishing for a job that had limits. A forty-hour week, specific procedures and tasks to be accomplished, a steady and regular pay check. A job that she could leave at the office when 5 o'clock struck. She bit a fingernail unconsciously and wondered if there was a job somewhere in real estate like that.

ANNE

As I painted my verbal mural way back in Chapter 2, the brush next touched Anne, Rubenesque and bold. Her voice is too loud, her vocabulary too colorful, her laughter too coarse. Somehow, you think, she doesn't quite belong in the picture. But she does. She has been selling real estate for seventeen years, she's good at it, and she likes it. And what's more, the real estate community likes her. The word is out that under the mask of big, brusque babe is a caring, generous, and competent woman.

Anne is the daughter of Polish immigrants, one of nine children. She has cleaned houses, worked on an assembly line, and waited on tables to support herself and her family, and she has always done the best that she could do. It was that line, "I always do the best I can do" that tipped the scales when she answered an ad for real estate sales agents. The broker had serious doubts that she would even pass the state exam, but he needed salespeople and he agreed to sponsor her.

Anne not only passed the exam, but turned out to be one of his hardest workers and most successful agents. But she never learned to care about fashion, or style, or even appearance. In fact, new customers were sometimes put off by her appearance and manner, and certainly some were lost, but those who stayed through a day were loyal and accepting.

Anne most often ran into problems with qualifying and negotiating, not realizing that many people guessed from her appearance and speech that she was uneducated, and therefore were somewhat reluctant to divulge financial information to her. In almost every working relationship, she had to overcome this prejudice and prove her knowledge and competence; yet it never occurred to her to change, to strive for a WASPy image.

And Anne broke all the rules, all the good advice for efficiency as a sales agent. Her calendar was also her desk blotter, doodled and noted upon so that dates disappeared among the maze of lines by the end of each month. Her appointment book was no book at all, but scraps of paper stuffed in her pockets "so she'd remember." (And of course sometimes she forgot.) But people remembered Anne, and they came to her and asked for her.

She was always busy, but she never had a problem in limiting the amount of time she spent working. Her natural love of life, all of it with all its pleasures, was sufficient to limit her working hours.

TERESA

Anne is talking with Teresa, a diminutive Hispanic, who also grew up in a large and poor family. But Teresa went along another road. She finished high school and got a job as a file clerk when all her friends were getting married and having babies. She went to business school and learned typing and secretarial skills and worked afterwards for five years as a secretary in a large corporation. She married a junior executive, was divorced two years later, took another secretarial job, and then discovered painting.

As her skill as an artist developed and her love for painting grew, Teresa began to resent the nine-to-five hours of her job. She longed for daylight hours to paint, but she needed an income on which to live. She saw real estate sales as a means to both goals.

Today she is a good agent, not especially aggressive and not candidate material for the top salesperson of the year award, but thorough and competent. She makes a comfortable income. She also takes at least three days off each week to paint, and usually works both days of every weekend. It is a life-style that exactly suits her needs.

JOAN

I painted one of my characters as a middle person, one who would go unnoticed in the aisles of a supermarket, and her name is Joan, kind of a "middle" name, don't you think?

Joan is a nice person, and I would bet that every reader of this book knows a nice person much like her, outwardly at least. She is in her forties. Last year the oldest of her four children entered college. Real estate sales for Joan was a way of re-entering the job market two years ago when she and her husband realized that college costs loomed ahead.

She chose the career primarily for the lure of flexible hours, but also because she was seeking supplementary income, income not needed for day-to-day living. She knew she could work on a commission basis without worrying about weeks or months passing without a check. Half a dozen sales or listings a year would pay tuition costs and fulfill her purpose in working.

Joan chose to work in a large franchised office because she wanted formal training and regular scheduled working hours. She did well at the training sessions and she does her work well, both in and out of the office. She follows the outlined procedures and complies with company policy. In fact, she likes having the bulky manuals on sales and listing procedures and techniques in her desk. She sees them as a handrail along the stairway of each deal. If she lacks the color of an Anne, or Doris, or Evelyn, she compensates in absolute reliability. She rarely makes waves.

Joan does not love real estate sales. She sees the work as just that, *work*, a job, and she performs its tasks well and thoroughly. She rarely takes the problems of her clients or customers home with her, although she is available for off-hours calls. She handles those efficiently, but will not let her job interfere with her commitment to her family.

Joan plans to continue working as a sales agent until her youngest child finishes college. And then? "It will depend," she says. "Commission money could pay for some pretty special vacations."

SALLY

Do you remember the redhead who was collecting dessert cookies? The one with the mud stains on the hem of her coat? This is Sally, the only one of the women on my mural who has children of grammar-school age and a toddler still at home.

Sally was torn between wanting to be a good full-time

mother, and wanting an identity and an income of her own. She thought selling real estate would be the answer to her two-way pull. If she could find a woman to baby-sit on the two or three weekdays that she had to work, she reasoned, her husband could take over while she handled weekend appointments. The job would also allow her the time off for parent conferences, and class plays, and school vacations, and days when a child was ill.

Sally found the job more difficult than she had anticipated, however, and the irregularity of the hours an extra burden as well as a cushion. She was about to give up trying to juggle family and career when she met Gail. Gail came to work in the same office four months after Sally, and Gail also had preschool children. The two young women became friends and hit upon the idea of a partnership arrangement where they would cover for each other on those we-need-you-at-once calls. They worked out a system of trading hours rather than money, and as a result have both not only survived in the business but also flourished. They are both happier at home because they work, and happier at work because they have time at home. And they remain very good friends.

ROBIN

I have yet to tell you about the youngest and oldest women in my mural. Robin is nineteen, the youngest. She's the pretty girl with the braid that comes almost to her waist, and she, like Anne, appears to be a little out of place in the group as you view the painting. But if the painting were a movie and you could listen to her talk, you'd know immediately that, appearances to the contrary, she very much belongs.

Robin is a college sophomore planning to major in real estate and currently working through a January internship as an assistant to a working residential agent. She likes the action of the job and she likes the idea of meeting and working with new people throughout the year. She likes the independence and lack of routine, and the flexible hours, of course. She has had, however, only one opportunity to witness a negotiating process in her three-week stay, and it impressed her with its complexity and intensity. It concerned her, too, mainly because she feared she would have to work especially hard to establish customer trust, to overcome the image that she's "only a kid."

But Robin is far from being "only a kid." In her career planning she is already looking beyond the residential sales agent's role that she is sampling this winter. Next year she hopes to apply for an internship in the administrative advertising departments of a large national franchise, and the winter after that she hopes to work with a commercial sales and leasing firm in a major city. She is determined to sample the career and explore as many aspects of it as she can.

In many ways Robin typifies the new attitude of young people toward a real estate career. In its *Membership Profile,* the National Association of Realtors states, "Few people enter real estate straight out of school. Fully eight out of every ten brokers and nine out of every ten sales associates had tried their hand at other endeavors before seeking their fortune in real estate." But that survey was conducted in 1977. Today as more and more schools and colleges offer majors and graduate degrees in real estate, and as franchising turns a once "Ma and Pa Office" business into big business, and as the giant multi-office corporations grow yet larger and more numerous, the profession is becoming almost as attractive as working for Exxon, or A.T.& T., or I.B.M. with the added advantage that it offers the opportunity to start and run one's own business at almost any given point and with minimal financial investment. Many states in the nation even waive the years of apprenticeship required for a broker's license if an applicant has a Bachelor's degree with a major in real estate. And many students have recognized that four years of college is a minimal time requirement for a ticket into a fast-growing and highly lucrative profession.

SARAH

Last but certainly not least I touch my brush to Sarah, the oldest woman in my painting. She is seventy-four, and has worked most of her life as an English teacher. She and her husband retired nine years ago to a condo community on the coast of Georgia and bought themselves a luxury motor home to explore the country leisurely. After three years, they were both bored and longed for something to do. The appeal of real estate was the unscheduled (and unlimited) vacation time and the chance to supplement their savings and retirement income with commission money that would allow them to travel in style.

They found an independent broker who accepted them as a team. Neither puts in a full work week, but together they are full time.

There are some problems, of course. Sarah gets tired after half a day climbing up and down stairs in six or seven houses, and she will not accept more than one showing customer a day. If there is another call and Hal, her husband, cannot or does not wish to take the customer out, Sarah has made arrangements to turn her leads over to other members of the office staff, receiving a referral fee of 10 percent of the agent's share of the commission if the lead results in a sale.

She and Hal schedule long vacations during real estate's slow periods (from November to mid-January and July and August) and they take long weekends during the other times of the year. Before they leave each time, however, they arrange for another member of the sales staff to cover, agreeing upon the financial compensation dependent upon the particular stage a transaction or customer is in. (A deal that is complete but awaiting closing would call for a minimal courtesy fee to compensate for the time involved in attending the closing; a customer who had been out with Sarah twice but had not yet found anything appealing would be turned over as a referral.)

Strangely enough, Sarah faces a working problem somewhat similar to that of Evelyn, Anne, and Robin. Each of them must overcome the prejudicial initial response many customers feel toward their appearance. In Sarah's case, the problem is age. Old in America often equates with worn out, broken down, and inefficient, and Sarah must demonstrate her energy, efficiency, knowledge, and competence again and again. She is very much aware of the situation, however, and handles it with a good deal of spirit.

Interesting people, aren't they? Each has different needs and goals in her real estate career, and each handles her job and its problems and demands in a slightly different manner. You may not have seen yourself as any of these people, or you may have seen bits of yourself in several characters. It doesn't matter; just glimpsing these people brings a realization of the shared and the separate rewards and problems of women in this business.

But now look at yourself. Who is the person you see? Why does she want to work in real estate? What are her goals? What does she want in her life?

When you see yourself clearly and answer those questions firmly and honestly, you will be on the road to success, real success in your job and in your life. Through understanding a career and its demands and understanding yourself and your needs, you will be able to merge the two toward your own continual growth and happiness as a person and as a woman.

TWELVE

Other Directions

"THIS is the last chapter," you are thinking, "the one that ends 'and she lived happily ever after.'"

Not quite.

Good endings—endings that leave you satisfied like the right dessert after a meal—are very much dependent upon their beginnings and the goals and limits that those beginnings set forth. The opening pages of this book promised you a guide to a successful sales career. For all those who have read it with that goal in mind, the book really should have ended with the preceding chapter, "A Woman First," with its stories of success and fulfillment in that career.

But I know that some women did not, could not, find an ending in that chapter. Perhaps, in the final analysis, they find sales work unfulfilling, or perhaps their individual personalities lead them always to reach a goal and ask then, "What next?" For these women, this book needs one more chapter, a chapter that offers the possibility of many new directions and that ends without a sense of finality. For them, and also for all those who want to know, just for the sake of knowing, let's look briefly at some other directions in real estate.

BECOMING A BROKER

You can earn and possess a broker's license and still perform all the roles and functions of a sales agent. Rather than sales associate, your card will probably read broker associate, but as such you can remain an independent contractor associated with a firm in the same way as the sales agents. In fact you will probably be asked to sign an agreement stating that you will not take listings or advertise property in your own name, but will act only on behalf of your employing firm.

The essential advantage of getting a broker's license is freedom. You can leave the firm with which you are associated at any time to start your own business, or if the firm itself should go out of business, your license remains valid without the necessity of a sponsoring broker.

Some states and some larger realty firms require a broker's license for holding the post of office manager. And getting a broker's license is also a good idea if you plan to move often during your career, since there is more reciprocity among states at the broker's license level than at the sales agent's.

OFFICE MANAGER

If you accept a post as office manager, you will begin to move out of sales and into management. Most office managers do, however, retain the prerogative to seek listings and make sales. Although they rarely canvass, they often do participate in caravans and Open Houses in order to stay on top of the market by being aware of what is for sale, at what price.

By the time an agent becomes an office manager, she will usually be getting a good number of referrals from former customers. Most office managers find it easy to take referred listings and they usually handle them as their own. Handling referred buyers, however, is much more difficult since showing and selling involves considerable time away from the office. In order to function effectively in their administrative role, therefore, most office managers assign buyer referrals to a sales agent who, they feel, will be able to devote the necessary time and care to the house-hunting process.

As an office manager, you will probably receive a regular salary in addition to any commissions you may earn from your own sales or listing work. And many offices pay their office managers an agreed-upon salary plus a percentage of all the commissions earned in that particular office. Sometimes there are even bonuses at the end of the year.

If lack of a steady income is one of your problems in a real estate career, office management might solve it. You will always know that your salary will at least meet your basic needs, and then your share of the office gross commissions (depending on how good business is) will make life easier or perhaps even elegant.

As an office manager, you will be expected to supervise the activities of both the sales staff and the clerical staff. This will include making and enforcing floor-time schedules, holding meetings, assisting in negotiation, mediating disputes, writing advertisements for listings, ordering supplies, and checking all material submitted to the MLS. If you have a broker's license and are given the responsibility, it may also include signing (taking) listings for the firm. If you are not a broker, you will probably be responsible for getting the unsigned listing to the broker for his/her signature.

Your job may also include training new sales agents if you work in a smaller and unfranchised firm. And if the firm is particularly small, it may include some bookkeeping, typing, and even cleaning up and painting or decorating.

The hours of an office manager are more regular, with less night and weekend time. They are also usually greater in number; few managers put in less than a forty-hour week plus, and sometimes the plus is a lot. Also, there will be less flexibility in your working schedule than you experienced as a sales agent. You cannot just decide on a week in Bermuda or an afternoon off to give yourself a break; you must make advance arrangements with the owner of the firm or its management staff. And you will find yourself covering for absent salespeople or filling in on schedule conflicts, which means that you may have to open houses for inspectors, show buyers a day's tour, attend closings, and run contracts over to lawyers or mortgage officers.

Perhaps one of the most important functions of the office manager is assistance with financing. Here you must never lose touch with the financial marketplace. Financing is one of the most difficult and complicated aspects of real estate to learn, and it is the one most quickly lost when not used and actively studied. As office manager, you will contribute much to your firm and your customers and clients by spending several hours each week studying mortgage trends and getting to know key personnel in all the local lending institutions.

In your new administrative role, you will frequently be asked to help fill in the blanks on a contract or offer form. In fact, in some offices the offer form or contract cannot be presented until the office manager reads through it. Since real estate offers can turn out to be binding contracts, the responsibility of checking them over requires some knowledge of real estate law and the self-assurance to refer customers or clients to an attorney when questions arise that you cannot answer adequately.

CORPORATE EXECUTIVE

Ten years ago if you had said "I want to be a real estate corporate executive," most people would have laughed. Today it is not only a possibility, it is a promising career. More and more students in colleges and universities across the country have their sights set on executive positions with the real estate corporate giants which are beginning to appear and grow in the United States.

The largest of these giants is Coldwell Banker, which was begun by two men in a small California office in 1913. In 1979, the firm consisted of 165 residential offices and 32 commercial offices. It employed 7,100 people.

On the East Coast, Coldwell Banker's newest rival is already a giant called Merrill Lynch Realty Associates, based in Stamford, Connecticut. Besides the name, with its connotation of reliability and fortune in the stock market, one of the contributing factors to the phenomenal growth of this corporation is its policy of buying an 80 percent interest in the leading local real estate firm in carefully selected and researched areas.

Each of these firms and others, smaller now but growing, offers the possibility of working in executive and highly specialized positions. In fact, the job of office manager and many of the specialties discussed in the following pages are but rungs on the corporate ladder in these companies.

RELOCATION SPECIALIST

This is a career for the city person, for it is particularly around the major metropolitan areas of the country that the huge multi-office firms are proliferating and only they can afford to pay a salaried specialist in relocation. These large real estate firms actively seek the business of handling corporate transferees for the other large corporations in the area, and the relocation specialist works closely with corporate personnel offices and officers.

If you choose this specialty, you will very rarely sell houses even though you possess an active salesperson's license, but you may show a great many houses as you conduct clients through their introduction to an area. You will meet your clients at an appointed hour at your office for their first consultation. There you will interview the family in order to establish their price range, preferences, and life-style, and then try to advise them as to which communities will best meet the majority of their needs and wishes. You may drive them through these communities yourself, sometimes showing properties that are for sale, or you may accompany a sales agent through the properties selected for the first day or two.

Your hours will be regular and so will your pay check. As a relocation specialist or adviser, you will forfeit most of the chances for a big sale or a big year, but you will be performing a service that is much needed and appreciated by uprooted families in this fast-paced world.

If you accept a job in an already established relocation department, you will find the step-by-step procedure of your work pretty much established for you. Your challenge will be in learning to interview people effectively and in matching them to the communities that best suit them. If you accept the job in a company where the position is a new one, however, you will face a creative and challenging task. In each of the company offices, you will be responsible for gathering community information, perhaps putting together booklets on community activities, maintaining contact with officers of local service and recreation groups, and keeping and updating lists of physicians, dentists, baby sitters, lawyers, etc. You will travel from one of your company's offices to another setting up a system of presentation for each of the towns it serves. Sometimes you may even take photos or make video tapes.

Relocation specialist is a job for an outgoing, active person who genuinely likes people. It stimulates an active social life, requires a high degree of community involvement, and leads to speaking engagements and special presentations.

FINANCING SPECIALIST

This is another job found only in the largest companies. In smaller firms every agent is, and must be, a financing specialist. Where the position is open, however, it is a challenging and exciting one, requiring an interest and aptitude in math as well as tact and compatibility with people.

Most of all, however, the job of a financing specialist requires the great patience and the special clarity of thought and expression found in every really fine teacher. Financing is complicated even to professionals; its intricacies must be untangled with the greatest care for the average home buyer. The professional financing specialist must lead them step by step through the process of judging which mortgage is best and then through the questions and answers of the application form. Sometimes the job also requires a little verbal muscle to help get things moving and cut through the red-tape snafus of a lending institution, and sometimes it requires a kind of intuitive leap to choose the "lender most likely . . ."

Working as a financing specialist has a regular work week and pays a regular salary, not related to commissions. There are occasional headaches and disappointments and occasional tense moments (hours or days, really). The paperwork sometimes seems endless, and accuracy and attention to detail are absolute essentials of survival. There are also many warm and sincere thank-yous as reward.

PROFESSIONAL TRAINING SPECIALIST

This career path is found primarily among the large franchises and the largest multi-office firms. As a professional training specialist, you will work for the franchise office or the corporate headquarters, not the individual member firm or office. Your job will entail teaching new agents and new member firms company procedures and the use of special sales tools and techniques.

To qualify for the position, you must have several years successful experience as a sales agent and all the qualities of an effective teacher. You must know residential real estate thoroughly and you must have the ability to keep a class moving and interesting, to involve all its members in the discussion, and to use sophisticated video-tape equipment in evaluating an individual's sales and listing effectiveness. You must also be able to tell a student what he or she is doing wrong in such a way that their self-esteem remains intact while they improve.

The hours and salary of a training specialist are regular and dependable if not spectacular. Some people, however, move from actual teaching into writing and creating the teaching programs, a step usually considered to take them into the corporate executive level. This job usually requires some travel, extensive research and reading, and the ability to function well in meetings. It also demands a creative mind open to new ideas, and an ear sensitive to the connotations and effects of particular words and phrases.

PUBLIC RELATIONS

A recent headline in our local newspaper read MUSIC IS INSTRUMENTAL TO SALES ASSOCIATE. The story told of a local real estate sales agent who was a musician, composer, and church organist. It discussed her family and her hobbies, and several times it mentioned the name of the firm for which she worked.

Was this a personality profile by an interested local reporter? Hardly. The article appeared in a section of the newspaper captioned REAL ESTATE HAPPENINGS, under which was written in much smaller print, *Articles submitted by advertisers.*

Throughout the country there is a movement to identify the real estate agency as a community service profession, and good public relations (P/R) work is essential to building this image. Larger firms and the franchises are, therefore, employing full-time associates to handle the job of getting the firm's name in the newspapers. Service articles on such topics as buying and selling of houses, energy efficiency inspection, new and proposed local development, and the awards and achievements of sales agents are the tools that the P/R specialist employs to help promote the company.

Public relations work also involves speaking before local groups and teaching "how to buy or sell houses" seminars. It is a job with regular office hours (on paper) that often spill over into homework and special assignments at odd times. It requires a flair for writing and speaking, a reporter's nose, and a creative mind.

Besides larger real estate corporations and the franchises, there are also positions for public relations people in local and state Realtor Boards and in the National Association of Realtors. Trade publications are produced at just about every level and all of them need experienced agents to write and edit, which means that your real estate career may lead to a magazine or newspaper job. This in turn may lead to writing on the topic of housing for the nationally circulated magazines or the book trade, but competition at this level is incredible and there are truly but a few spots open.

There is also a movement within the National Association of Realtors and another movement among the executive planners for public television to produce educational programs on real estate similar to the much-acclaimed *Wall Street Week*. Both groups are considering series programs to be broadcast on a regular basis over the course of a viewing season, and both are aiming for late 1981 or 1982 as starting points. Script writers will of course be needed as well as panel members and guests.

COMMERCIAL LEASING AND SALES

All of the previous "other directions" that I have mentioned are related to residential real estate. They are offshoots of the residential sales job and essentially none of them harbors or hides prejudice against women. Commercial real estate, however, has been traditionally a man's field. (Women didn't even begin to break in until the mid 70s.) That is not to say that a woman didn't occasionally lease some floor space, or sell a commercial tract of land, but few—extremely few—women specialized in commercial transactions.

Why? It's big business, big money, and a very different ball game from residential sales. Commercial brokerage focuses strongly upon leasing space for stores, offices, warehouses, factories, and other businesses. The leases are often complicated and just as often take months to negotiate. The numbers involved are mind-boggling: a $500,000 deal is considered very small and the commissions start at 6 percent and move upward.

Like it or not, the customers are almost exclusively men, and extremely successful businessmen at that. There has been and still is considerable distrust and uncertainty about women as commercial agents, and to do well in the field, a woman must prove herself again and again against difficult odds and unvoiced prejudices. She must be aggressive, competitive, very competent, articulate, and very much at ease in a masculine world. The competition in the field is unrelenting and there is no room for feelings or good-guyness.

Most commercial brokerage specialty companies or offices are located in large metropolitan areas. Most agents start in the smaller companies and move to the larger ones after some years of experience. But the large commercial houses are not totally opposed to new people and sometimes have excellent training programs. A woman must impress her interviewers as knowledgeable, intelligent, dedicated, articulate, and tactful. She must be willing to persevere to the end of a negotiation through sometimes incredibly tangled jungle with demanding and unyielding customers and clients on both sides.

The income of women who make it in commercial brokerage is high, sometimes in the six-figure range. It is high-pressure work, however, and requires nerves of steel and a cast-iron stomach, good going-to-sleep ability, and no emotional hangups about rejection or the quality of one's competence. The hours are more regular than residential sales since they are more or less limited to the business week, but it is no place for a part-timer.

Commercial real estate is a career for a career-centered woman who is dedicated to excellence, and determined to achieve financial success. It demands great patience and a good deal of vision. It demands a sense of self-worth strong enough to approach complete strangers in executive positions with proposals and ideas that are new and might even be considered offbeat. It demands the ability to speak up and speak clearly; the ability to direct without pushing; the tact to know when to hold back; and the intuition to know when to present a new approach.

PROPERTY MANAGEMENT

Everywhere across the country condominiums are "in." Their incredible popularity has prompted the growth of another career option for women, property management. Until the last decade this also was an exclusively male domain. In the mid-seventies, 3,071 men but only 117 women held the designation of Certified Property Manager (CPM). Today the number of women in the field has doubled and doubled again, and is still increasing at a rate much faster than for men.

Especially among larger residential management firms, women are becoming recognized for their ability to handle people. And that's just what the job requires. Not only handling tenants and condo owners, however, but also handling maintenance crews, deliveries, accountants, tax assessors, special repair crews, etc., etc.

This is a job that does not necessarily require a real estate license. You may work for a property management firm in which you will be one of a number of account executives, each assigned a number of properties to manage. Or you may work directly for the builder/developer of a complex, or for the owner's association of a condo or a co-op. Sometimes you will be given an apartment to use on the premises if you choose to manage a single property. Or you might consider opening your own property management firm. Then you might manage condos, co-ops, multi-family houses, and even single family rentals. You would also have to staff your office and manage the people who worked for you.

Commercial property management differs somewhat from residential management and has been even more exclusively a male domain, but slowly women are becoming interested and attracted by the income and variety of the job. It includes managing shopping centers, office buildings, and huge rental complexes or "cities" where there are both commercial centers and residential apartments. The work involves leasing units, supervising and arranging maintenance activities, and sometimes planning special events. It also quite often involves the arbitration of grievances between tenant and tenant, or between tenant and landlord.

Property management, both residential and commercial, does not offer the high potential income of commercial brokerage, but on the other hand the pay check is steady, the tension less frequent and more manageable, and the demand for competent people increasing. The Institute of Real Estate Management awards the designation Certified Property Manager and has available a number of books and pamphlets on the career and its demands and opportunities. Write or phone:

Institute of Real Estate Management
National Association of Realtors
155 East Superior Street
Chicago, Illinois 60611
[312] 440-8630

The National Center for Housing Management is a non-profit office which was established by Presidential Executive

Order in 1972. They also have career information available. Write:

National Center for Housing Management
1133 Fifteenth Street N. W.
Washington, DC 20005

APPRAISAL

I have a friend who is an economist, and from time to time I beg a professional opinion or two. He is generous with his time and knowledge, but he never fails to remind me that economics is an inexact science and that economists are not known for their accuracy. Most appraisers would also agree that appraisal is an inexact science, but few would add that members of their profession are not known for their accuracy. In fact, appraisers like to believe that, given the opportunity, three appraisers evaluating the same property would each quote a figure within 5 percent of the other two. And surprisingly enough the majority of them do.

There is a maxim in real estate that says a property is worth the highest price a ready, willing, and able buyer will pay and the lowest price a ready, willing, and able seller will accept. In other words, property value is dependent upon a meeting of the minds. This of course presents the essential problem for the appraiser since she must determine that dollar figure without the buyer or seller present to guide her.

Learning the work of an appraiser takes time and much experience. Like real estate sales work, all the training manuals in the world can't replace on-the-job experience. In fact, the American Institute of Real Estate Appraisers requires five years professional experience in appraising along with other qualifications before granting its designation MAI (Master, Appraisal Institute).

Appraisers generally work for lending institutions, the federal, state, or local government, very large real estate firms, or specialty appraisal firms which are sometimes called fee appraisers. Fee appraisers usually work on a free-lance basis—that is, commission or payment for specific work done. Other people in the field usually work a nine-to-five, five-day week, with a salary.

Appraising has been another traditionally male stronghold, and the number of men in the profession still far outstrips the number of women. But women are entering the field, and they are encountering less prejudice and opposition than in commercial leasing and sales. If you enjoy the financial evaluation part of real estate but not the selling part, this may be a good avenue to explore. For more information you might contact:

American Institute of Real Estate Appraisers
155 East Superior Street
Chicago, IL 60611
or
Society of Real Estate Appraisers
7 South Dearborn Street
Chicago, IL 60603

OPENING YOUR OWN OFFICE

There are some one-man real estate offices still in existence in the country and some of these are in actuality one-woman offices. Usually these people work out of offices in their homes and usually their income is relatively small.

More and more in today's business world, real estate is becoming a highly specialized professional field. Running your own office usually means joining the National Association of Realtors, the state and local Realtor Boards, and the local Multiple Listing Service. Yes, there are some people making it as discount offices or special service brokers (for example an all rental office) but their numbers are few and the failure rate is high. There is also increasing pressure across the country to join one of the large franchises in order to compete with the multi-office corporations.

Opening your own office means first of course that you must be a licensed broker. It also means the investment of both time and cash in the beginnings of a business. You must purchase or lease a building or floor space, furnish it, stock it with the necessary papers, contracts, letterheads, etc., and have enough capital for several months running before commissions begin to come in.

You must also attract sales agents to work for you, train them, and learn to manage them. You must learn advertising. You must establish a trust account to handle deposit monies. You must find a lawyer to represent you and an accountant to manage your bookkeeping and taxes. And most of all you must be willing to step into a highly competitive business and work endless hours to get your business rolling.

It's another world. You have stepped out of sales and into independent business management. And that's another book.

I wish I could give you more than these fleeting glimpses of what a TV commercial might call the "Wide Wide World of Real Estate," but perhaps they are enough to start you thinking and searching. Or perhaps they are enough to assure you that residential sales is exactly the right career for you.

INDEX